By the same author

The Penguin Guide to
Freshwater Fishing in Britain and
Ireland

compiled by Ted Lamb

The Penguin Guide to Sea Fishing in Britain and Ireland

for shore and boat anglers

ALLEN LANE

ALLEN LANE
Penguin Books Ltd
536 King's Road
London SW10 0UH

First published 1983

Filmset in Monophoto Univers by
Northumberland Press Ltd, Gateshead
Printed in Great Britain by
Richard Clay (The Chaucer Press) Ltd, Bungay, Suffolk

Lamb, Ted
   The Penguin guide to sea fishing in Britain and
   Ireland.
   1. Salt water fishing—Great Britain—History
   I. Title
   639'.22'09   SH457

   ISBN 0–7139–1577–3

To my wife Catherine, and Zebedee and Octavia

Contents

Acknowledgements

My grateful thanks to all the people who supplied the detail necessary to complete this guide and gave advice and guidance on the sort of information that would be welcomed. Special thanks also to Bob Page of the National Federation of Sea Anglers, whose help has been invaluable for many years, and to the tourist boards of Northern and Southern Ireland. Final thanks to my family, without whose forbearance the task could not have been completed.

Introduction

There are big differences between a guide for freshwater fishing such as *The Penguin Guide to Freshwater Fishing*, which is a companion to this book, and a sea fishing guide. One of the most obvious differences is the fact that, with very few exceptions, sea fishing is free.

To linger on that point for a moment: during the early 1980s, moves to introduce a national sea fishing rod licence reached the early stages of becoming law. Thanks to the intervention of worthy bodies like the National Federation of Sea Anglers and the National Anglers' Council the moves were blocked. However, this does not mean that they will never reappear.

The fact that sea fishing is free, apart from minor charges for fishing from municipal and private piers and jetties, and charges for boat hire and the like, means that lengthy lists of fishery owners are not needed. So why a guide?

The sea angler moving off his own ground, or the inland sea angler with a choice of many locations, needs to know the nature of the shore or offshore mark where he is to fish; additionally he needs to know sources for bait, tackle, and perhaps boat hire. More important, though, he needs to know what sorts of fish are likely to be encountered. Freshwater fish are, as it were, trapped in their environment, while the movements of sea fish are seasonal. The big bream shoals which delight the summer angler on the south coast vanish to warmer climes in the winter, to be replaced by cold-water species like the cod.

This guide aims to put all this information at the angler's fingertips, as well as listing the spots which are recognized locally as good fishing marks, capable of giving rewarding sport, together with notes about the fishing methods which are most productive.

Before You Fish

Bait collecting

Details of known bait grounds are given in the guide, but anglers should be careful about worm digging on holiday beaches where local by-laws protect interference with carefully tended sand. Very often there are nearby alternative sites where digging will not affect anyone's enjoyment. Many resort tackle shops stock worms dug by local professional bait-gatherers, and other sources are fishmongers and fish markets in fishing towns. See also pp. 109–10 below.

Shore safety

Shore fishing in several areas holds dangers unless you know the sites intimately. Gently sloping beaches with a great deal of distance between low and high tide marks can see the unwary cut off, as can rock outcrops scored with deep gullies. Take extra care in these areas. See also pp. 96–9 below.

Night fishing

The dangers mentioned above are amplified at night. Besides taking great care not to get cut off, a strong, wind-shielded light is necessary, plus extra clothing in case of bad weather or low temperatures.

Boat comfort and safety

Very often a fine, warm day on the shore can be a chilly experience when you leave the shelter of the coast and you find yourself exposed to wind and weather. Extra clothing is a must. So is life-saving gear, provided on most charter boats by law. Young people should wear lifejackets, as should everybody when there is a likelihood of rough weather.

It is inadvisable to go out on your own unless you know with certainty the local tides and impending weather. Charts for the area should be carried, together with a compass, in case of fog, and some means of warning larger shipping of your presence, such as a whistle or loud bell. Know the capabili-

ties of your engine, too, for a water with a strong tide rip like the Humber estuary has seen many an amateur boatman unable to make headway home.
See also pp. 104–6 below.

Booking boats

With the increasing numbers of sea anglers, pressure on charter boat booking is heavy, especially through the summer and more especially at weekends. Trips involving a charter should be booked well ahead, and, because of the uncertainty of Britain's weather, an alternative date should be given if at all possible. The boatman's word is law if he refuses to go out or offers an inshore trip rather than risking his boat in a gale. The charter skippers advertising regularly in the national angling press all offer a high standard of fishing in Board of Trade registered boats. Those who return consistently good catches are likely to be booked heavily.

Protecting fishing

Digging holes in beaches has already been mentioned. Fill them in afterwards, for holes filled with water are a danger for unsuspecting walkers and waders, especially children. Take only as much bait as you need, and, if you overturn boulders, replace them to protect the creatures, especially immature bait, underneath them. Litter should always be taken home and disposed of, especially discarded nylon line, which is a hazard to wildlife.

Immature fish

Please return to the water any immature or small fish. This protects future stock. Also return alive and unharmed any fish which you do not want. One of the saddest sights I have seen was a little pile of chequer bass, five or six inches long, left on a quayside in Plymouth by some unthinking angler. Given a few years they would have made four- or five-pounders.

The Areas Covered in the Gazetteer

The coastal waters of the British Isles have been divided here into thirteen broad areas in order to give first an overall picture of the coastline of each region, the species which visit it and the times when they appear.

Within each region the guide moves along the coast, treating individual fishing locations in detail, with notes on how they can be reached, tackle, bait and boat-hire availability, and the sorts of fishing methods used.

The regions are:

GAZETTEER

One

North-East England

Northumberland to the Humber

The North-East and North Yorkshire mean codling to most anglers, with the peak of the fishing during the winter, especially after storms and during very cold weather – factors which drive the North Sea's vast cod stocks into coastal grounds. Fish on the whole are of moderate weight, from 2 lb upwards. Fish of 10 or 12 lb are taken, but these are rated very good indeed. While it might be expected that anglers concentrate on cod from late summer through to spring, there is good flounder fishing from December to February in estuary areas, notably the Tyne. Other species include coalfish and pollack, while increasing numbers of plaice are being taken in localized marks on mussel and worm baits. Lug remains a favourite bait, with mussel running close second. In the shallower water south of Flamborough Head to the Humber there are tope, dogfish and whiting.

On the colliery beaches of Durham and Northumberland, setting for many winter shore matches, long casting with weights of 6 oz and up produces the best results. In general the more steeply shelving waters which give better depth are best.

Flamborough Head and the rocky shoreline of Yorkshire are handled differently, and not without some danger. Anglers here may perch on ledges high above the water to drop leads into the deep scours which lie close in. Steady nerves are needed, and the novice should be wary. Codling are the usual reward.

It should not be imagined that summer fishing is a waste of time, for in many parts the codling stay all year, and night fishing is often rewarding.

Summer bass fishing is improving, too, especially from Flamborough south to Spurn Head, and thornbacks are present.

Not a great deal of boat fishing takes place, and boats which do go out tend to concentrate on inshore marks. However, tremendous potential exists for fishing over the rocky ridges and wrecks, all largely unexplored, off this productive coastline. Exploratory trips have yielded good ling and conger in addition to the coastal species.

Berwick-upon-Tweed

Northwards to Burnmouth and Eyemouth lies an excellent codling beach culminating in rocky sections. Flatfish and whiting are also taken. To the south is Spittal Beach running into Redshin Cove, offering similar sport. At Black Rocks (codling, whiting) there begin the extensive shallow waters inshore of Holy Island, where flatfish are the mainstay, with codling and whiting on high tides. Spittal Beach, Huds Head, Bear's Head and the North Breakwater are rated best locally. There is a tackle shop at Berwick. Bait can be dug on the beaches, with the North Breakwater area productive for lug. Angling boats put out from Eyemouth, to the north.

Beal
Gives access to the Holy Island causeway, a large area of shallow water. Flatfish mainly. Lug plentiful. It is signposted off the main A1 road.

Ross
Gives access to the southern, marshy end of this area.

Bamburgh
The B1340 runs southwards along the coast here to Seahouses and rocks starting by the lighthouse at Carr End, extending to Bentall and Beadnell Bay. Codling, whiting, flatfish and mackerel. Lug fairly easy to find. Bamburgh is signposted off the main A1. Tackle is available at Seahouses, where there is a pier and harbour and boats can be hired for fishing around the Farne Islands. Conger and dogfish are taken in these waters in addition to the shore species. Fishing the deeper water beyond the Longstone can offer big cod, monkfish, haddock and rays.

Boulmer
Linked to the B1339; gives access to the rocky area at the north of Alnmouth Bay. Good codling ground. Best bait area is Alnmouth estuary.

Alnmouth
Codling, whiting, flatfish and mackerel from the beaches, with good numbers of flounder in the estuary in winter. The estuary is also a good bait ground. Boats are available for fishing the bay, where catches are reasonable.

Amble
Lies at the southern end of Alnmouth Bay and is off the A1068 road. Two piers offer excellent flatfish sport and summer mackerel. Worms can be dug in the harbour, where boats can be had to fish the offshore water for codling, coalfish, pollack, haddock, thornbacks and flatfish. Best-rated local spot is Hauxley Point. To the south lies Druridge Bay, accessible at Chevinton Drift, off the A1068. Flatfish, codling, thornbacks. There is also a road from Widdrington to Cresswell giving access to the bay.

Lynemouth
From Lynemouth north to Cresswell lie The Scars, below which is deeper water offering good codling fishing, coalfish and flatfish. Offshore pollack, rays and dogfish can be taken. To the south is a good stretch of beach fishing followed by more rocks at Beacon Point, which is accessible from Newbiggin.

Newbiggin-by-the-Sea
Good mixed fishing, with codling predominating in winter from Beacon Point in the north to Cambois along the coast road southwards. The river mouth at North Seaton offers plentiful worm bait and good flounder ground.

Blyth
Codling, flatfish, eels and gurnard are taken from the West Pier, and the beach fishes well for codling and flatfish, which are taken upriver as far as the ferry. Bait is easily found. The A193 road joins the coast here, running south to Whitley Bay.

Seaton Sluice
Lies at the north end of Whitley Bay. Good flatfish and codling. Bait easily found.

Whitley Bay

From St Mary's Island down to Culler-coats and the Tyne estuary, Whitley Bay offers good codling fishing, especially in winter, when it is the scene of huge sea matches with entries of thousands. Other species are whiting, eels, flatfish and occasional rays.

South Shields

The A183 runs along the coast south-wards from here to Sunderland past Marsden and Whitburn. Codling, flatfish. Fishes best in winter after storms. Bait grounds at Whitburn Bay provide lug and rag. Tackle shops in South Shields and Newcastle.

Whitburn

Codling and whiting. Good bait ground. Access from here to the north end of Roker.

Sunderland

Beach fishes well for codling and flatfish, also some coalfish, but storms can put it out of bounds by flinging the lead back. Boats go out, with the main catch codling, whiting and coalfish. Piers and wall fish well when the beach is out of action. Another good local mark is Grangetown. Average codling about 5 lb. The Wear estuary can be rewarding. Tackle shops in Sunderland. Whitburn Bay is the best bait ground, and the estuary.

Ryhope

On the A19 road south of Sunderland. Rock edges give flatfish and billet to 2 lb. Can fish well for rays.

Seaham

Off the A19 road. Shore fishes well for codling and flatfish to Beacon Point, where rays are also a feature. Tackle

shops. Boats available, with cod, had-dock, rays and whiting offshore. Average cod around 6 lb. Pier and groynes pop-ular marks. Bait can be obtained locally from shops.

Easington

A good beach for codling and flatfish, reached by the A1086 north from Hartlepool.

Hartlepool

Billet and codling from shore and piers to 4 lb. Boats are available, the main offshore catch being codling to 6 lb. Local marks include Heugh Breakwater, Lighthouse Corner and North Gare. Tackle shops provide bait. Hartlepool Bay is good flatfish ground with shallow water extending from the Tees estuary. The A178 gives access to the estuary and Seal Sands, where gullies can give flounders at high tide.

Tees Bay

Good flatfish ground round to West Scar, accessible from the A1085. Codling can be good on big tides. The estuary provides good worm ground, also peeler crab, which can be a telling bait for codling and flatfish. Tackle and boat hire at Middlesbrough.

Redcar

From here southwards the coastline alters to a series of bays broken by rock outcrops. Access is a little more difficult south to Whitby, and on to Scarborough, where the coast is served by roads branching from the A174 and A171 roads. Redcar beach and rock edges fish well for codling, with some whiting, haddock and flatfish. There is a tackle shop providing bait at Redcar. South Gare breakwater can fish well.

Marske-by-the-Sea
Reached by the A1042 south from Redcar; gives good rock edges and beach fishing for codling and flatfish. Bait available locally.

Saltburn-by-the-Sea
Offers similar fishing to Marske. The pier here can fish well, and a good local mark is the edge of Saltburn Scars for codling. Bait available locally.

Staithes
The rock edges fish well here for codling and flatfish, with some whiting. Worm, peeler and mussel good baits.

Kettleness
Off the A174. Rock edge fishing for codling and flatfish.

Whitby
Beach fishes well for cod from 2 to 3 lb. Pier can be affected by floodwater from the Esk but at other times provides flatfish and codling. Bass are a feature of this region, more and more being taken in recent years. There are tackle shops providing bait (lug and mussel best), but it can be collected in harbour at low tide. This is also one of the premier boat-fishing stations of the North-East, and offshore catches include good cod, haddock, conger, dogfish, pollack, plaice and rays. There are mullet in the harbour region in summer. Other good local marks are Robin Hood's Bay and Sandsend. Robin Hood's Bay is reached by a road branching from the A171 south of Whitby at Hawsker.

Staintondale
Off the A171; gives access to Ravenscar and South Cheek, also Cloughton Newlands and Cloughton. Some deeper water can be reached from these areas, and they provide good codling fishing.

Scarborough
This famous resort has good rock fishing at the Basin, East Pier and the Horseshoe. Bass are again a feature of catches, and there are also codling, coalfish, flatfish, mackerel and whiting. Marine Drive sands fish well for flatfish. Boat marks include South Bay (codling, flatfish) and Scalby Mills rocks (bass). Boat catches also include conger, pollack, haddock and some ling. Tackle and bait available in local shops.

Gristhorpe
To the north of Filey; offers good beach and rock edge fishing.

Filey
Flatfish are the main sport in the bay, but good tides can bring in codling in numbers. Coble Landing is a good mark, also Cayton Bay. The rock fishing along Filey Brigg is famous, not least for the skills of the participants in keeping out of the water. Stations on the rocks include Crab Hole, High Brigg, Binks Gulley, High Nab and The Pulpit. Besides winter codling the rocks give coalfish, pollack, mackerel, flatfish, whiting and wrasse. Boats are available, and the most popular marks are the rocks off Flamborough Head and the water under Bempton Cliffs. Locals rate mussels and razorfish (both easily obtained) the best bait, but fish are also taken on lug, which is easy to dig or can be obtained from tackle shops in the area.

Flamborough Head
The major promontory of this coastline, it can be reached by taking the B1229 or B1259 off the A165. Major sport winter codling. Offshore boat fishing, with boats from either Filey or Bridlington, can be very rewarding.

Bridlington

Bridlington Bay is at the head of a long, almost straight shoreline stretching south to the hook of Spurn Head. The main species from rock and beach marks in the bay are codling and flatfish. The north and south piers can fish well for codling and flatfish. Boats are available for fishing the water to the south of Flamborough Head, which is a broad ribbon of largely shallow water stretching down to the Humber mouth. Besides flatfish and codling, boat marks offer thornbacks and whiting. There are good worm grounds in South Bay and on the outer banks. As at Filey, local anglers rate mussel bait highly. Some tope and bass in bay.

Hornsea

Reached by the B1242, which stretches south from Bridlington right down to Withernsea. The shore fishing is not highly rated, but codling and some thornbacks are taken. Boats offshore take tope in addition to flatfish and thornbacks, with occasional bass. Worm from beaches. Tackle shops also supply bait in Hornsea. South from here to Withernsea there is access to the shore at Mappleton and Tunstall. Creeks provide flounder fishing on winter high tides.

Withernsea

Shore catches include bass and conger besides codling and flatfish, with some thornbacks. Offshore catches are better and include skate and some tope, also dogfish. There are plentiful mackerel in the bay in summer for bait, while worm is easily dug on beaches or can be had from local tackle shops.

Spurn Head

The B1445 branches from the A1033 east of Withernsea to reach Easington, where a smaller road serves Kilnsea and runs on to the head. Kilnsea Corner is a good mark on the head, where shore fishing provides codling, flatfish, conger and silver eels, bass and skate. Boat fishing off the head can be good, with boats available at Hull. Some tope have been taken here. Bait is plentiful along the shore.

North Humber

Codling, flatfish, eels and pouting are taken along the estuary and its creeks. Worm is plentiful. Boats can be hired at Hull for fishing off Spurn Head (see above). The Humber runs strongly on the ebb, and boat owners should be careful that they have the engine power to make port again, or should arrange to return on a flood tide.

Two

North-West England and the Isle of Man

Cumbria to the River Dee

The North-West coast differs from the North-East in that there are no large rocky areas, and, overall, there is less deep water. A marked feature is large, shallow bays with considerable areas of exposed sand and mud at low water. As might be expected, flatfish are abundant, and there are chances of dogfish and tope for boat anglers.

In common with the North-East, however, the codling fishing can be extremely good during winter, and there seem to be many more large cod in recent years. Whiting, from October to March, are a lot more plentiful than on the North-East coast; piers are the best shore access to these and the codling. Skate are sometimes taken from the shores but are more likely to be taken from boats. The southerly piers, such as Southport, also produce some bass and gurnard in the summer. Some resort piers are closed to anglers through the summer.

There are localized worm grounds for bait, but on the whole worms are not plentiful and the visitor is advised to bring some or order some in advance. Fish strip can be a useful alternative along this coast, where it is rather more popular than in the North-East.

During winter, which undoubtedly offers the best fishing, the coast has a wild and exposed beauty, especially when rapidly changing weather is racing in on westerly gales.

Moving to the Isle of Man: The sea fishing off the island is superb, with large skate, sharks (mostly blue), conger and tope taken from boats – even beaches in some parts. The beaches in general offer flatfish and cod, with many opportunities for bass. Other species include ling and pollack.

As with shore fishing in the North-East, long casting pays off from North-West beaches. A two-hook rig, with a lower small hook baited for dabs and other flatfish and a larger upper hook with a biggish bait for cod, is a good bet. From the piers, paternoster rigs are popular.

On the Isle of Man, fish come fairly close inshore and there is some deep water. Paternoster rigs are popular here, with float rigs for rock fishing. The larger offshore species like tope, shark and skate require specialist tackle, which is often supplied by charter boat skippers.

Bowness-on-Solway
The Solway Firth abounds in flounders, so much so that they are often thrown away as useless by the salmon trappers who work the estuary. Bowness is off the B5307, which also gives access to Glasson and Cardurnock on these waters at the extreme end of Hadrian's Wall. Cod

and whiting are taken on spring tides backed by a westerly. Bait is plentiful and tackle is available in Carlisle.

Silloth

The B5302 from Wigton gives access, and from here south to Maryport the B5300 runs along the shoreline. The area is relatively underfished, but there are flounders with cod on night tides.

Maryport

Reached by the A596. Maryport promenade can fish very well indeed for codling of 2 to 3 lb, and an average winter catch might be 10 or 12 lb of fish. Allonby Bay, to the north, gives skate, plaice and dabs. Lugworm and fish strip are favoured locally.

Workington

The pier is a good bet for small codling and whiting. Favoured local shore marks are Harrington and Lowca, both producing good cod, especially on night high tides. Boats available, many working north to Allonby Bay, which gives the added chance of skate and plaice. Tackle shops in town.

Whitehaven

Moss Bay to the north provides whiting, codling and flatfish, with some thornbacks for dinghy anglers. The shore is good for winter codling and whiting at night. Again, the codling are on the small side but can be plentiful. Tackle and bait in town.

St Bees Head

Accessible through St Bees, off the A595 trunk road. This is the major promontory of the coast, and there are some deep spots fairly close in for dinghies. Codling, whiting and flatfish make up most catches. To the south lies a long stretch of fairly straight coast, accessible through Nethertown, Sellafield and Seascale, all off the A595.

Drigg

By the mouth of the River Irt. From here to Ravenglass the shore fishes very well for codling and whiting, with lug the best bait. Some may be dug locally.

Kirksanton

Lies on the A5093 across Duddon Sands from Barrow. Nearby Silecroft and Haverigg give access to shore fishing, with flatfish predominant. Off shore there are tope and skate, with hire boats available at Barrow. Mussel and worm bait from local grounds on the sands.

Barrow-in-Furness

Good local marks include Scarth Hole, Piel Island, Foulney Island, Roa Island and Black Tower on Walney Island, also the deep-water berth at Walney Channel. Shore fishing gives mainly whiting, cod, flatfish and some rays, with offshore fishing giving a chance of tope. Tackle shops and bait in town.

Morecambe Bay

The principal catches in the bay are codling, whiting, dabs and plaice. During the summer there are also bass, tope and some conger, best approached by dinghy. Tackle and bait from Morecambe shops.

Morecambe

Shore and Stone Jetty fish well for plaice and dabs in summer, with codling, whiting and flatfish in the winter. Best bait worms and fish strip. Daylight fishing is often poor. Tackle and bait in town.

Heysham

Fishing as Morecambe (see above). Tackle and bait in town.

Fleetwood

Boats are available for fishing the coast and Morecambe Bay from Fleetwood, where tackle and bait are also available. Main shore catches are flatfish, with cod and whiting in the winter. Tope and skate are taken from boats from spring through summer, while winter provides mainly codling and whiting, on the small side but numerous.

Blackpool

From Cleveleys down to Lytham the shore offers only average fishing for flatfish and codling, but the piers can offer excellent catches, especially on winter night tides. Tackle and bait are available at the Central and North piers, also in the town. When fishing is slack inshore dinghies take codling and whiting about a mile out.

Lytham St Annes

Gives access to the River Ribble mouth, where the main catches are flounders and silver eels. Some codling and whiting on high tides. Bait grounds in estuary.

Southport

Among the species that have been taken from the extremely long pier are dabs, flounders, plaice, whiting, codling, sole, conger, gurnard, bass, mullet and skate, although in the main the first four species predominate, with codling and whiting the main winter catch. Bait can be dug but is available, as is tackle, in the town. While most local anglers concentrate on the pier, the extensive flats, miles of them dry at low tides, can give good flatfish on the flood. The shore is extremely exposed in bad weather, and the tide makes very quickly and could trap the unwary.

Wallasey

Fishing is largely ignored where the great and mucky Mersey discharges, but at the extreme end of the Wirral there are flatfish to be taken by enthusiasts. On the Dee side of the Wirral the picture begins to change, but the best fishing in the region is undoubtedly from Rhyl westwards.

The Isle of Man

Castletown

Both beaches and boats provide flatfish, cod, pollack, wrasse, tope and conger. Rowing and motor dinghies are available locally, also tackle and bait. Grounds producing giant skate, to 200 lb and more, lie just 600 yards off Langness. Summer fishing, from June through to October, gives the best sport.

Douglas

Victoria and Battery piers give plaice, sole, cod, dogfish, coalfish and congers through summer, with cod and flatfish mainly in winter. The same fish, plus wrasse, are taken in Douglas Bay. Douglas Head and Little Ness Head provide good sport with float tackle or spinning. Just half a mile out there are big tope, conger and cod. Boats, tackle and bait available locally.

Laxey

The beach fishes well for bass and also produces plaice and dabs. Flatfish and cod from boats. Summer fishing best, with mackerel usually plentiful.

Ramsey

Bass from Ramsey beach to Point of Ayre, with the best fishing in late summer. The beach and pier also provide flatfish, cod and conger. Tackle and bait in town.

Kirkmichael

As on the east coast, the bass fishing is good in late summer from Point of Ayre down. Spinning and bait fishing are popular. Flatfish and dogfish are also taken from the beaches, where blue shark are sometimes contacted.

Peel

The breakwater gives excellent winter fishing for haddock, cod and flatfish and summer fishing for bass and coalfish. The beach provides bass and flatfish. Skate grounds, also producing flatfish, lie 400 yards off White Strand in Peel Bay, with the best fishing in summer. St Patrick's Isle offers good rock fishing. Tackle and bait in town.

Port Erin

An excellent boat station for the big skate, tope and shark off the Calf of Man. Catches also include pollack and flatfish. Shore fishes best for flatfish. Tackle, bait and boats locally.

Port St Mary

Like Port Erin (above), a good boat station for the shark and skate grounds. Tope, cod, conger and ling also feature in catches. Rocks and pier provide pollack, coalfish and wrasse. Tackle, bait and boats locally.

Three

East Anglia and South-East England

The Humber to Margate

East Anglia is one of the most rewarding areas for winter cod fishing in Britain. At night, when the cod are moving in, mile upon mile of anglers' night lamps can be seen along the beaches, and a winter night's catch might be ten or so codling up to 5 lb, with very good chance of better fish of 10 lb or more.

While all the beaches produce fish, those which are steeply shelving are rated best, since they give access to deep water without the need for extra-long casting. However, long casts even here seem to provide better sport. Large worm baits are used with cod in mind, the best being a bunch of lugworm, perhaps tipped with tougher material like squid or fish strip to hold the worms in place for a long cast.

Other fish present in winter are flatfish, especially in the Humber and Wash areas, where thornbacks are encountered. Summer fishing provides flatfish, thornbacks, mullet and bass. The latter, while not numerous, are often big. At the tail end of summer whiting can be expected, sometimes in numbers. The piers are popular, and from some of these large stingray are taken in most summers. There are plenty of opportunities for boat fishing, with good grounds for all the above species fairly close inshore.

From East Anglia southwards, the summer fishing improves and there are more and more opportunities for boat fishing, where species taken further south in the Channel can often feature in catches – bream, conger, and various kinds of dogfish. The whole of this area can produce tope, some very big, which are most likely to be taken from boats.

Worm bait suppliers are abundant, although it is usually practical to dig your own from the many productive grounds unless weather or time dictate otherwise. Mackerel are normally plentiful during summer.

One of the most welcome features of fishing in the South-East is the effect of the campaign to clean up the River Thames. Year after year the fishing in this area improves, and several species are re-establishing themselves.

Grimsby

An excellent boat station for fishing the deeper stretches of the Humber out towards Spurn Head, which offer dabs, flounder, plaice, pouting, cod and conger, with some thornbacks. Grimsby's pier and the shore provide flatfish and codling in the main. Bait is plentiful on estuary shores. Tackle available in Grimsby, where charter boats can be organized. Some of the small land drains and creeks running into the estuary provide flounders and silver eels. North Wall fishes well.

Cleethorpes

The beach can give good codling and coalfish on high tides during winter and mainly flatfish in summer. Bait available on the beach south to Saltfleet.

Saltfleet

Access here and further south at Theddlethorpe St Helen (both off the A1031 south from Cleethorpes) to winter codling fishing and summer flatfish. Bait can be dug locally.

Mablethorpe

Codling, whiting, coalfish and flatfish from the shore here and at Trusthorpe and Sutton-on-Sea south towards Skegness on the A52. The shore is best after a good winter blow. Tackle and worm bait available in Mablethorpe.

Chapel St Leonards

The sea wall fishes well for codling and flatfish, with the added attraction of some summer bass, sometimes big fish. Lug plentiful on local grounds.

Ingoldmells

Between Chapel St Leonards and Skegness. The sea wall here is the best bet on good tides. Codling and flatfish are the mainstay, with a chance of bass. Bait and tackle from Skegness.

Skegness

Beach and pier fish well for codling, whiting and flatfish, with summer bass from the town out to Gibraltar Point, at the northernmost corner of The Wash. Tackle and boat hire available, also bait suppliers in town, although the beach has worms for the digging.

The Wash

The shallow, and therefore rather treacherous, waters of The Wash hold good stocks of flatfish, skate, tope and dogfish, with cod in winter. A boat from Skegness gives access to the deeps off the north shore. Dinghy anglers have to be especially wary of moving sandbanks, and even careful local anglers are sometimes stranded. The tidal mouths of the waters running into The Wash – the Nene, the Ouse and the Welland among them – all offer excellent winter flounder fishing, and every so often sea-trout are taken by flounder fishermen. One noted flounder (local name 'butts') spot is beneath the main road bridge in the town of King's Lynn.

Heacham

Codling and flatfish from the shore. Dinghies offshore also take rays, dogfish and tope. Sandbanks can be a menace. Bait can be dug locally.

Hunstanton

Local favourites are the beach from the slipway to the cliffs, the promenade and the pier. These offer flatfish, thornbacks and occasional good bass. Boats offshore take cod and rays, but again in this area there is a danger of hidden sandbanks. Some big stingray have been taken off Hunstanton. Worm bait can be dug on the beach and tackle is available in the town. Brancaster Bay and Holkham Bay, to the east towards Cley, are accessible from the A149 at Burnham Norton, Overy Staithe, Holkham and Wells-next-the-Sea. They offer good shore fishing for flatfish and rays, with some winter cod and whiting.

Cley-next-the-Sea

Cley has a steepish shingle beach which is popular for winter cod and whiting and conger, bass, mullet, pollack and flatfish at other times. Bait is difficult to find here, and the best bet is the grounds at

Blakeney Point to the west. Local shops also stock bait and tackle. Boats are available, and offshore catches include black bream (summer) and turbot. The harbours at Blakeney and Morston can fish well for flatfish and mullet.

Sheringham

Less shingly than Cley, the beach here gives codling and whiting in winter, with flatfish, including some turbot and brill, rays and bass during warmer months. The steepest beach is Old High, which is a good summer night mark and can produce during the day in winter. Tackle is available in Sheringham, also bait. Worms can be dug from exposed sand at low tide. A few boats for hire.

Cromer

Cromer beach and the pier fish well for codling and whiting in winter, with summer bass, rays and flatfish. Offshore catches include conger, coalfish, dogfish and tope. Tackle is available in town, and there are worm grounds opposite the lighthouse. From Cromer running south-eastwards, the A148 gives access to the shore at Sidestrand and Trimingham, offering similar fishing to Cromer.

Mundesley

Can be a very good winter cod spot from the beach, with flatfish in the summer. Thornbacks and tope are also taken. Worm can be dug at low tide.

Bacton

Another noted cod shore, with a chance of bass in summer. Worm suppliers locally, with some to be dug at low tide. The B1159 running south to Caister gives access to the shore at Happisburgh, Sea Palling, Waxham and Winterton.

Winterton-on-Sea

With Newport, Scratby and California, gives access to the shore adjacent to Hemsby Hole, a tongue of deeper inshore water bordered by sandbanks. The shore gives cod and flatfish, while a dinghy over the hole can produce good catches of thornbacks. Some lug from low-tide banks.

Caister-on-Sea

Good winter cod and whiting fishing down to Yarmouth, plus flatfish in season. Offshore marks give good mixed fishing, and summer catches include bass and bream, gurnard, dogfish, rays and tope. Bait available locally.

Great Yarmouth

Piers and beaches here give good fishing for cod, whiting and dabs in the winter, with flatfish, rays, bass and other fish in summer. Best local choices are the harbour mouth, South Beach, Wellington Pier, the jetty, Britannia Pier and North Beach. Boats available locally for good mixed fishing, including bream, tope, rays, coalfish, dogfish and gurnard. Bait suppliers in Yarmouth.

Gorleston-on-Sea

Good mixed fishing, as at Yarmouth. Some good bass are taken from time to time, also rays, tope and dogfish, the latter three species best approached by boat from Yarmouth in the deeper water of Yarmouth Roads. Access to the shore further south at Hopton and Corton, where a favourite local mark is Tramp's Alley. Some bait can be dug, or there are suppliers at Yarmouth and Lowestoft.

Lowestoft

Catches include cod, whiting (winter), flatfish, mullet and bass. Local favourites are Claremont Pier, North Beach, Pakefield Beach, South Pier and the waters off the harbour, which are best approached by boat. In addition to the above species boat anglers take tope, rays, dogfish, conger and ling. Bait is supplied locally, but some may be dug. Boats available for hire or charter. Tackle shops.

Kessingland

Can be a good winter codling beach. Offers good mixed fishing at the Lowestoft shore spots (see above). Some bait locally, or from Lowestoft.

Southwold

Favourite local spots include the harbour and pier, Eastern Bavents, Gun Hill car park area and Covehithe. Shore offers cod, whiting, flatfish, mullet and bass. Boats are available locally and give access to tope, dogfish, conger and rays. Bait and tackle available in Southwold.

Sizewell

Access to the shore here and further south at Thorpeness, through Saxmundham. Codling and whiting (winter), flatfish and thornbacks, with a chance of bass. Bait and tackle from Saxmundham. The shore at Dunwich, between Southwold and Sizewell, offers flatfish and can be good for cod in winter after a blow.

Aldeburgh

The shore fishes best for flatfish, with cod in winter months, also whiting. Good tides bring in fairly big cod, and in summer there is a chance of thornbacks. Bait can be hard to find but is available in the tackle shop at Saxmundham. Fish strip and worm are favourite baits.

Bawdsey

Gives access to the southern end of Hollesley Bay, which gives fair catches of winter codling and whiting, with flat-

fish through the summer. The approach is along the B1083 from Woodbridge. Some worm at low tide. Tackle and bait obtainable in Felixstowe and Ipswich.

Felixstowe

Boats are available here for hire or charter, and they offer the best fishing, especially off Cobbold's Point. Bass, cod, whiting, flatfish, rays and tope are taken. Occasional tope are also contacted from the shore in addition to the other species. Cobbold's Point is also a good shore mark, together with the beach northwards to Bawdsey, Felixstowe Ferry, The Dip, Manor End and the town pier. Bait and tackle available.

Harwich

Harwich Harbour fishes very well for rays and flatfish, with cod and whiting in winter, and the accessible fishing in Dovercourt Bay offers the same. Boats, tackle and bait are available, and some worm can be found in Dovercourt Bay. Boats give access to very good fishing for bass (some big), conger, cod, whiting, rays and tope.

Walton-on-the-Naze

Frinton beaches, the long pier and Naze Tower offer bass, cod, whiting, mullet, flatfish, dogfish, rays and tope. Boats are available in Walton or Frinton, giving access to very good tope and ray fishing, with big cod in the winter. Stingray are also fairly common. Good boat marks include West Rocks, North-East Gunfleet, Medusa Buoy and Cork Sands. Mackerel are usually plentiful in summer, and worm and tackle are available in Walton and Frinton.

Clacton-on-Sea

The pier and beaches provide summer flatfish, rays, some tope, angler fish and bass, with winter cod and whiting. Jay-wick sea wall and Holland Haven are reckoned good bets for winter fishing. Offshore catches include rays, tope and turbot. Tackle and bait available locally.

Brightlingsea
Flatfish and, in winter, codling and whiting, usually plentiful, along the Colne estuary and upriver. Some bass and mullet also taken in summer. Lug-worm fairly easy to find.

West Mersea
Mainly flatfish, with plentiful winter codling and whiting. Stingray also taken. Worm plentiful.

Bradwell
Boats are available here for hire or charter, and they give good access to rays, tope, bass and flatfish, with excellent winter cod and whiting fishing. Bait available.

Burnham-on-Crouch
Flatfish and some bass and mullet, with winter codling and whiting in estuary. Bait plentiful.

Southend-on-Sea
Pier and beaches running from Leigh to Shoeburyness give summer bass, flatfish, conger, tope and wrasse, with good winter fishing for codling, whiting and flounders. Boats are available, giving access to tope and ray grounds and also pollack and black bream marks. Tackle and bait available in resorts, but worm may be dug locally.

Gravesend
High tides, especially those backed by easterlies, bring some bass in summer and cod and flounders in winter. North-fleet Creek produces flounders, with some summer mullet. Worm and tackle available locally. Best local marks are foreshore from Greenhithe to Gravesend, Sea School and Cooling beaches. A local speciality bait for codling, whiting and flatfish is cooked shrimp. Best boat marks are Grain Edge and All Hallows.

Sheerness
Good fishing here and at Warden Point and Leysdown-on-Sea for summer bass and mullet, flatfish, rays, dogfish and silver eels, and winter codling and whiting. Eel and flounders in the Swale, with some bass. Good tope grounds off the island. Bait and tackle available locally.

Herne Bay
Reculver and Swalecliffe beaches offer the best shore fishing, and bass, mullet, flatfish, dogfish, pollack, eel, tope, turbot, cod and whiting are taken. Grounds a mile off Swalecliffe, Pansands and Copperas Channel give consistently good returns for boat fishermen. Herne Bay Pier can be very good for winter codling. Boats for hire and charter; tackle and bait locally.

Margate
Access to nearly ten miles of beach, although this can be crowded during the holiday season. Minnis Bay can give very good catches. Cod, whiting, bass, mullet, flatfish and tope are taken from the shore, while boats give access to red and black bream grounds, rays, turbot, dogfish, gurnard and pollack and good winter cod fishing. On shore, the rocks sometimes produce the larger cod. Boats available in Margate, also tackle and bait. Worm can be dug at low tide.

Four

The South Coast and the Isle of Wight

Ramsgate to Lyme Regis

It is difficult to generalize about the Channel in fishing terms, save to say that it is blessed by lying between the North Sea, noted mainly for its splendid winter cod fishing, and the warmer waters of the Western Approaches, where, besides ling, bass, pollack, coalfish and conger, there are numbers of the larger sharks and, from time to time, stray exotics like the sunfish. A mixture of North Sea and South-West species spreads throughout the Channel, but there is a marked influx of winter cod towards the eastern end, off Kent and Sussex, from October onwards. If the Channel has any one speciality, it is the shoals of bream which move to off-shore stations during summer. What they lack in size, black and red bream make up for in spirit, quantity and edibility, and their arrival is eagerly awaited.

The coast, with its famous resort beaches, is broken by numerous ports and harbours, and a huge choice of boat fishing exists. For the beach fisherman, night fishing, rock fishing and the remoter beaches give refuge from summer holiday crowds, as do the harbours and breakwaters. Tackle shops are numerous, and most supply bait in some form.

Inshore trawling has made inroads into Channel fish stocks in recent years, with bass particularly suffering, but in general fishing is very rewarding.

Fishing methods vary according to the location: harbours and jetties lend themselves to paternoster ledgering and float fishing, while spinning can be rewarding in both locations and from beaches and rocks. When mackerel shoals are close in, a trace of feathers thrown well out and drawn swiftly back near to the surface can sometimes give dozens of fish in minutes. On the gentler beaches long casting gives the best results, but there are good steep shores, like the immensely long Chesil Beach, where deep water lies close in. On most beaches, night fishing on a high tide is usually best. A range of baits is useful, lugworm and ragworm being the universal first choice, followed by fish strip, squid strip, peeler crabs and shellfish. Most of these baits are available at coastal tackle shops, with some worm grounds for digging your own (although this resource is diminishing as some grounds become worked out by professional and amateur diggers). The fishmonger is a useful back-up but catching mackerel for a boat trip is usually no hardship.

Ramsgate
Bass, flatfish, mackerel, garfish, conger and turbot, with good winter cod and whiting fishing from the shore at Pegwell Bay and the Stour estuary, Western Undercliff and Marina Slopes. East and West piers also good shore bases. Boats

for hire or charter, giving access to shark, red and black bream, skate, conger, dogfish and turbot, as well as big winter cod. Tackle and bait available locally.

Deal

Similar summer fishing to Ramsgate, with excellent winter cod fishing with fish to 20 lb. Good spots are the pier area of the beach, Sandwich Bay and Walmer, just to the south. Bass and flatfish will often stay into winter. Best baits are cod and squid, with sprats a favourite for whiting. Boats, tackle and bait available locally.

St Margaret's at Cliffe

Good shore fishing in St Margaret's Bay, especially for winter cod. Rocky South Foreland also productive. Tackle and bait available locally.

Dover

There are excellent choices of shore vantage-points in Dover, where summer catches include black bream, bass, conger, pollack, mullet and flatfish, with cod (sometimes very big) from October onwards. The bass can also be big and often stay late in the season, with smaller fish year-round. While the beaches from here to Folkestone all offer reasonable sport, the harbour beach, the Southern Breakwater, the Admiralty Pier and Prince of Wales Pier are local favourites. With tides running, the outer vantage-points require fairly heavy tackle and leads. Boat fishing out from Dover (local hire available) gives bass, black bream, conger, gurnard, cod, dogfish, sharks, rays, turbot and tope. The Varne bank (15 m) is a favourite mark. Bait and tackle available locally.

Folkestone

Superb wreck fishing extends from Folkestone to the far south-west, boats (available locally) taking bass, cod, flatfish, rays, conger, bream, angler fish, pollack and other species. The Varne bank (15 m) is also accessible. The beach and pier also offer good fishing for a variety of species. Good winter cod venues are Sandgate Castle, Riviera Rocks, Prince's Parade and Harbour Pier. Bait and tackle available locally.

Hythe

The beach and rocks off Sandgate give good catches of bass and flatfish, with cod and whiting in winter. The Military Canal outfall is another favourite spot. Boats from Folkestone take black bream, cod, conger, rays, tope and flatfish on grounds off Sandgate. Tackle and bait available locally.

Dymchurch

Good shore fishing in St Mary's Bay, with catches including bass, flatfish and some rays, with cod and whiting from late summer. Local bait grounds.

Lydd-on-Sea

Gives access, via the B2075 from New Romney, to Denge Beach and the Dungeness promontory. Long casting here can get a bait into deep water, and Dungeness has produced excellent cod catches. The bass fishing, once famed in the area, with shoals drawn by the warm-water outlet of the power station, has declined in recent years because of off-shore netting. Flatfish are also abundant. Favourite local marks are The Dustbin, Diamond, and the Black Post at Broomham. Some bait locally.

Rye

Rye harbour offers flatfish, mullet, eels and some bass. Good mixed shore fishing from Winchelsea Beach nearby. Worm available locally.

Hastings and St Leonards

Shore catches include bass, flatfish, cod and whiting. Favourite local marks are Hooks Hard, Fairlight, the Town Pier, Goat Rocks, St Leonards harbour wall, The Gulley and beach from Harbour Arm to East Groyne. Boats are available, giving conger, dogfish, pollack and tope in addition to the above species. Bait and tackle available locally.

Bexhill

Good boat and shore fishing for bass and flatfish in summer and cod and whiting from October. Tackle and bait locally.

Eastbourne

Shore fishing at Pevensey Bay, Langney Point and Beachy Head gives bass, cod, eels and flatfish. Black and red bream, with some pollack, are additional species to be taken from Eastbourne pier. Boats are available for offshore bream fishing and winter cod fishing. Rays, tope and turbot are also taken by boats. Tackle and bait available locally.

Newhaven

Birling Gap, Cuckmere, Newhaven and Seaford beaches give bass and flatfish, with cod and whiting from late summer. The Ouse estuary is popular for mullet and flounders. Other marks are Tide Mills, Martello Tower, Salts, and Newhaven West Arm. Mackerel, worm and squid are used locally, available at tackle shops in town. Boats are available; catches include black bream, angler fish, pollack, ling, conger and tope in addition to the above species.

Brighton

Beaches at Russell Street, Banjo, Medina and Norfolk give bass, flatfish, mullet, conger, cod and whiting. Other marks are Black Rock, Banjo Groyne and rocks at King Alfred Beach. The Palace Pier is open for fishing from October to March and gives good catches of cod and whiting. Boats are available for grounds giving conger, ling, pollack, gurnard, angler fish, rays and tope in addition to the above species, also black bream. Tackle and bait available locally.

Hove

Beaches give bass and flatfish, with cod, whiting and rockling from late summer. Bait and tackle locally or in Brighton.

Worthing

Beach and pier fish well for bass, flatfish and mullet, with codling and whiting in winter. Flounders and mullet in mouth of River Adur at Shoreham-by-Sea. Boats, bait and tackle available locally.

Littlehampton

Boats out from Littlehampton take very good catches of bream, conger, ling, mackerel, gurnard, skate and rays, turbot, tope, bass, angler fish, cod and whiting. Beaches and groynes are fairly productive for shore species, with good bass and mullet fishing in the mouth of the River Arun. Winter flounders are also abundant here. Tackle and bait available locally.

Bognor Regis

A boat from Bognor provides bream, bass, angler fish, cod, conger, dogfish, rays, tope, turbot and whiting. The edge of the inshore reef can be productive; it is also a danger to boats at low tide, and care must be taken. Better grounds are through the shipping lanes, a trip which also requires care in fog (I know, I was fog-bound in an 18-ft dinghy here, which was none too pleasant). Excellent fishing for shore species on high tides at Pagham Beach, Felpham Beach and

Bognor Beach. Pagham harbour can also be good. Pier closed to anglers. Boats, tackle and bait available locally.

Portsmouth and Southsea

Bass and flatfish, with pouting, whiting and codling in late season from shore marks. Favourite spots are Gilkicker Point and Haslar Wall. Hayling Island, to some extent a refuge from holiday crowds, is a good summer choice. Boats, available locally, give access to very good winter cod and whiting grounds and, in summer, oceanic shark, skate, bream, bass, pollack, tope and turbot. Bait and tackle available locally.

The Isle of Wight

The island was the first south-coast venue to attempt fishing for the large oceanic sharks, formerly attempted only in Cornwall. Catches have been rewarding and this sort of fishing is on offer from island ports. Boat catches also include bream, bass, pollack, coalfish, cod, ling, mullet, wrasse, tope and flatfish. Excellent shore fishing, especially rock fishing, abounds on the island, and there are opportunities for float fishing, spinning and ledgering for a variety of species.

The Solent

Bass, bream, cod, conger, flatfish, garfish, ling, mullet, pollack, tope and wrasse taken from shore marks such as the Solent harbours and anchorages, Lepe Beach, Park Shore and Hurst Castle beach. Offshore catches include cod, sharks, conger, monkfish, bream, tope and turbot. Bait and tackle available locally.

Lymington

Fishing for main shore species from Lymington river mouth, Barton and Milford beaches and at Hurst Point. Bass to late season. Lymington offers charter boats giving access to bass, cod, conger, shark, tope, rays and flatfish. Tackle and bait available.

Bournemouth

Shore fishing good from Hengistbury Head, Poole Bay, Boscombe, Sandbanks and Southbourne. Main catches are bass, flatfish, mullet, codling and whiting. Piers at Bournemouth and Boscombe also fish well. Boats, available locally, give access to shark grounds as well as bream, dogfish, pollack, rays, tope and turbot. Tackle and bait available locally.

Poole

Main shore species taken from Sandbanks sea wall, Parkestone Bay, Hamworthy Beach, Evening Hill and Baiter, with mullet, flatfish and some bass from Poole Harbour. Plaice fishing here can be very good. Boats are available, giving access to bass, cod, conger, dogfish, sharks and turbot. Tackle and bait available locally.

Swanage

The pier and beaches offer good fishing for main shore species in this area, while boats give access to bream, bass, coalfish, cod, conger, dogfish, flatfish, pollack, shark and turbot. Boats, bait and tackle available locally.

Chesil Beach

This long and, for the most part, steep-to beach offers fine fishing into deep water, although it invariably fishes best on good high tides at night. All the main shore species are taken, also bream. Bass fishing is best following storms. The mackerel shoals which work along the shore in summer can give excellent daytime sport by casting out a trace of feathers or, more sportingly, a small lure on light tackle. During storms the beach can be dangerous, and care must be taken. Bait and tackle from Weymouth.

Weymouth

A good point for fishing Chesil, with additional good shore fishing at Durdle Door, Preston Beach and Weymouth sands. Town pier and Stone Pier also good. Boats, available locally, catch angler fish, bass, bream, coalfish, monkfish, conger, dogfish, flatfish, shark, tope and turbot. Bait and tackle from local shops.

Bridport

At the western extreme of Chesil and West Bay, making a good point for starting to fish these venues. Good shore fishing for all main species, best after dark, especially to avoid holiday crowds. Boats are available locally to fish for angler fish, bass, bream, flatfish, conger, pollack, turbot, wrasse and whiting. Bait and tackle available.

Lyme Regis

Main shore species from Lyme beach, Western Beach, Church Beach and Church Cliff. Boats are available, and catches include bream, conger, angler fish, cod, dogfish, gurnard, bass, pollack, shark and wrasse. Mackerel usually plentiful, and worm bait available locally.

Five

South-West England, the Channel Islands and Scilly Isles

Devon, Cornwall, Somerset and Avon

Besides being a popular holiday area, the South-West draws many anglers with its excellent shore fishing and fine deep-sea angling over reefs and wrecks, or on the established or developing shark grounds. Because such a variety of species may be sought, and because the shoreline and offshore marks are so varied, the individual entries will have to speak for themselves. However, one can generalize to the extent of saying that the majority of anglers visiting this area would want to sample the shore bass fishing or take advantage of the superb deep-sea fishing offered by experienced and long-established boat bases. Summer provides the best of the fishing, but the offshore marks fish right through winter for such species as pollack, coalfish and ling (reaching their heaviest weights during the spawning period after Christmas), and shore anglers can catch bass late into the season and flounders and whiting in the colder months. Cod are present, but not in the numbers encountered in the Channel or in northern waters. They begin to be more numerous from the North Devon coast and into the Bristol Channel.

Sidmouth

Bass, bream, mackerel, garfish, wrasse and flatfish from the shore, with additional dogfish, turbot and whiting off-shore. Tackle locally, with worm and peeler fairly easy to find.

Budleigh Salterton

Good shore fishing, as Sidmouth (above). Tackle and bait available locally.

Exmouth

Bass, mullet, flatfish, bream, whiting and wrasse from the shore. Local marks are the pier and Old Jetty, Orecombe Point, Bull Hill Bank, and Shelley Gut. Boats available, giving pollack, turbot, conger, dogfish, cod and pouting in addition to the above species. Tackle available locally. Worm grounds on Shelley Beach, or from points along estuary. The sheltered water within the bar is good flatfish ground in storms, giving turbot, plaice and flounders, with some mullet and bass.

Dawlish

The angler based here has the choice of open sea-shore fishing or the protected Exe estuary in rough weather (the estuary has bait in abundance). Dawlish beach, backed by red cliffs, gives bass, cod, conger, pollack and wrasse, with good catches of mackerel when the shoals are in. Boat Cove Wall is another local favourite. Boats, available locally, give access to good bass, cod, conger, dogfish, pollack and tope around the outcroppings of red rock. Horse Rocks and The Wreck are also good marks. Tackle available locally.

Teignmouth

The beach and sea wall provide all the main shore species, while the estuary provides some of the best flounder fishing in the west during the coldest parts of winter – fish of 2 lb and more are fairly common, and although the bottom is snag-ridden, fishing is very worthwhile. Worm baits and peeler crab provide the best flounder sport, but a baited flounder spoon can be effective. Boats are available, giving access to good mixed fishing. Bait grounds above Shaldon Bridge. Tackle shops.

Torquay

Local shore marks for bass, mullet, flatfish, garfish, pollack (mostly small), coalfish, cod, whiting, dogfish and tope at Hope's Nose, Abbey Sands, Anstey's Cove, Maidencombe and Watcombe. Boats available locally for fishing in Babbacombe Bay and Tor Bay (bass, flatfish) and wrecks further off giving conger, ling, coalfish, pollack, bream, dogfish and turbot. Tackle is available locally, and there are worm grounds on Torre Abbey Sands at low tide. Harbour also good.

Paignton

Shore marks for main species include Hollicombe Head, Roundham Head, Goodrington Sands, Paignton Sands, Broadsands, Elderberry Cove, Saltern Cove, Churston Point. Boats are available, and good marks include The Ridge (pollack) and off Roundham Head (pollack, coalfish, bass, conger, dogfish). Tackle is available locally, and most of the beaches provide worms at low tide.

Brixham

Brixham is a noted deep-sea port for wreck fishing, most of its reputation being based on superb returns of very big congers and large catches of pollack, coalfish and ling. The boats also take sharks and turbot. Closer in, there is still superb fishing for pollack, bass and coalfish, with occasional good conger at Berry Head, Shoalstone, Seven Quarries, Penny Rock, East and West Cod Rocks, Mudstone Ledge and St Mary's Bay. Shore fishing can also be good for the main shore species. Popular venues are the Pier Head and Victoria Breakwater. Tackle available locally and worm at Broadsands.

Dartmouth

The Dart estuary is another excellent winter flounder fishing spot in this part of the world, well worth remembering when winter storms put boat fishing out of bounds. Other shore marks include Compass Cove, Blackpool Sands, Slapton Sands, The Embankment and The Castle. These all produce the main shore species. Boat fishing, available locally, gives access to The Skerries, a superb flatfish ground for plaice and turbot, with good black bream in early summer. There are also wrecking trips, and other boat marks include Blackness Rock, Castle Ledge, Homestone Ledge, Mewstone, Western Blackstone, Eastern Blackstone, Anchor Stone, Redgates and Bull and Combe Rocks. Worms and peeler crab from local beaches and the estuary.

Salcombe

Bass Rocks, The Bar, Poolstone, Bar Reach, Blackstone, Rickham Rock, Mewstones, Prawle Point, Meg Rocks, Lannacombe Bay, Gregory Rocks, Ham Stone, Poolworthy Point and Saltstone are good boat marks for pollack, conger, bream, coalfish, gurnard, shark, dogfish, turbot, monkfish, cod and whiting. The beaches at Salcombe harbour entrance fish well for main shore species, local favourites being Splat Cove. Lambury Point, Rickham Sand and Prawle Point. Tackle is available locally, and there are worm grounds along the estuary.

Bigbury-on-Sea

Bigbury Bay is an excellent bass water, especially for dinghy fishing. It also provides pollack and flatfish. Shore marks include Bantham Rocks, The Narrows and Sand Flats, with bass, pollack, flatfish, garfish and mackerel the main catches. Worm can be dug at low tide.

Newton Ferrers

Newton Ferrers, with Plymouth, makes an ideal base for deep-sea boats to reach the Eddystone Reef, besides many wreck spots. These give bass, pollack, coalfish, conger and ling as the main species. The harbour and River Yealm give bass, mullet and flounders and provide worm grounds at low tide. Tackle and boats available.

Plymouth

Another good access point for fine deep-sea wrecking and for fishing the Eddystone Reef, Plymouth can also offer sheltered fishing within the giant breakwater and in the Hamoaze when storms put the offshore grounds out of bounds. Other boat marks are off Rame Head, and Hands Deep. There is plenty for the shore angler, too, with the Hoe giving bass, small pollack, mullet, flatfish, mackerel, garfish and wrasse, the Plym and Tamar mouths giving bass, flatfish and mullet (popular spots on the Tamar being the floating pontoons below Saltash Bridge). The seaward side of the breakwater gives all the main shore species and is popular for contests. Sutton Harbour and the Barbican also give small coalfish, pollack, bass, mullet and flatfish. Several tackle shops and plentiful local bait – fish from the fish quay, worm from the estuaries (a good spot being near the Cremyl Ferry landing at low tide), and peeler from among the rocks at the west end of the Hoe and in the estuaries. West of Plymouth lies Whitsand Bay (sometimes called Whitesand Bay), which is an excellent bass and flatfish beach. The best spot is reached by cliff paths through the firing ranges to the south of the Millbrook–Crafthole road; local papers give times of access through the ranges, which should not be crossed when red flags are flying.

Downderry

Good bass, wrasse, mackerel, garfish and some pollack from the outer edges of this rocky area – without good knowledge these rocks can be dangerous. Portwrinkle Jetty can sometimes be good at high tide. Seaton Beach is good for bass and flatfish, especially after storm has built it up. Bait plentiful on small beaches and among rocks. Some tackle at village general shops.

Looe

The name of Looe is synonymous with shark fishing, and today it remains the headquarters of British shark fishing. Charter boats for shark fishing are well organized, and advance booking is advised. The blue shark is the main quarry, and usually the first to arrive in early summer. Threshers, makos and porbeagles are also taken. Wreck and reef charters are also possible from Looe, and even short inshore trips are usually productive for conger, pollack, coalfish and ling. Looe's Banjo Pier and the harbour can fish well at high tide, and some big catches of flounders, mainly to peeler crab, are made from the pier end. Looe's smallish beach fishes best after dark, especially in summer. The rocks produce bass and the main shore species, with big wrasse from time to time. Bait, both worm and peelers, is plentiful locally.

Fowey
The Fowey River can look very striking when china-clay washings run down the coast, with a marked division between the white river water and the blue of the sea. When the water is coloured, fishing is not too good from the shore. A high tide can pen it back up the river, and mullet, bass and flounder are taken up to Lostwithiel sawmills. Rock and beach fishing for main shore species at Crinnis, St Catherine's Point, Polruan, Polridmouth Cove and Par Beach, also Fowey Harbour and Albert Quay. Boats available for reef and wreck fishing. Tackle and bait available in town, or worm may be dug in the estuary.

Mevagissey
Beach fishing for main species at Port Mallon, Polstreath, Blackhead, Pannance and Porthpean. Excellent rock fishing too, with black bream and conger among catches. Outer harbour wall also fishes well. Perhaps the best rock mark is Dodman Point, and boats, available locally, have good mixed catches just off the point. Another good boat mark is Gwineas Rock. Tackle and bait available locally.

Falmouth
Penryn Harbour and the estuary provide bass, flounder and mullet. Falmouth is a good base for much rock and cove fishing over a wide area. Reef and wreck marks can be reached by boats, available locally, and catches include conger,

pollack, coalfish, ling, rays, flatfish, tope, dogfish, bass and wrasse, with good catches of black and red bream. Bait is fairly plentiful, with worms at low tide and peeler from rocky areas. Tackle available in Falmouth.

Coverack
Bass and mullet from the harbour and local beaches, with good mixed catches from rocky areas. An offshore sandbank, reachable with boats (available locally), gives good catches of rays and big flatfish. Rocks and wrecks provide conger, coalfish, pollack, ling, dogfish, bream, gurnard and other species. Bait available locally.

Porthleven
Mount's Bay gives fine bass fishing, and the beaches and rocks near Porthleven also provide their share of catches, together with main shore species. Boats and tackle are available locally, boats giving access to rock marks for conger, coalfish, pollack, ling, black bream, turbot, dogfish, gurnard and other species. Bait plentiful at low tide.

Penzance and Newlyn
Excellent rock and cove fishing in the area, especially for bass. Boats available, giving access to rock marks for good mixed catches of the main offshore species. Popular shore marks are St Michael's Mount, Treen, Ayr Point, Eastern Green, Logan Rocks, Loe Bar, Porthcurno and Sennen Cove. Newlyn's piers also give good catches. Worms are available at low tide from many beaches. Boats and tackle available locally.

Mousehole
Another good point for fishing Mount's Bay and the Lizard Peninsula, especially in westerly gales, from which it is sheltered. Good shore bass fishing, and

some boats available for rock marks like Runnel Stone and Longships. Tackle and bait available locally.

Guernsey, Channel Islands
Accessible by ferry from Plymouth and Channel ports, and air service from Exeter and Plymouth. The shoreline has many rocky points ideally suited to spinning and floatfishing for bass, mullet, pollack, garfish, mackerel and bream, with some very big wrasse. Boats available from many points by arrangement with local boatmen. Offshore grounds give skate and shark in addition to main species, with shark fishing becoming quite an attraction.

Jersey, Channel Islands
Accessible as Guernsey (see above). Plenty of rock, cove and harbour fishing in the area; the best quarries are bass, pollack, bream, and big wrasse. Piers at Bouley Bay, Bonne Nuit Bay, Greve de Lecq, Rozel and Gorey, also St Helier breakwater, give good bass and bream catches. Boats available in St Brelades Bay and some other points by arrangement locally. Bait plentiful and several tackle retailers.

Isles of Scilly
Boat service from Penzance; helicopter from St Just via Penzance. Plenty of good shore fishing, especially for bass, pollack and flatfish, the latter on sandy ground. Some boats available through St Mary's Boating Association, Hugh Street, St Mary's. Good deep-sea rock catches, especially on The Prowl, off St Agnes. Bait plentiful, with many shops stocking tackle.

St Ives
Moving around to the north coasts of Cornwall and Devon, the opportunities

for boat fishing decrease because of the more exposed nature of the coast, vulnerable to westerly gales. However, there are some superb surf beaches, giving excellent shore fishing for bass during the summer and autumn, with cod and whiting in winter. Flatfish, mullet, pollack, mackerel and garfish are also taken, with The Island and Godrevy Point being popular marks. Flatfish, mullet and bass also in the Hayle River. Boats available for reef and sandbank fishing with good mixed catches. Bait plentiful and tackle available locally.

Perranporth
Accessible by the B3285 road off the main A30 between Redruth and Indian Queens. Good surf fishing for bass and flatfish from Penhale Sands in Perran Bay. Bait at low tide. Some tackle available locally.

Newquay
Bass, flounder and mullet are main shore catches, with codling and whiting in winter. Good beaches are Fistral, Great Western, Crantock, Lusty Glaze, Porth Towan, Tolcarne, Whipsiderry and Watergate, with the harbour and promenade at Fly Cellars and Newquay's quays. Pentire Head, Towan Head and the Gannel estuary can also give good catches. Boats are available; catches include bass, conger, pollack, coalfish, black bream, dogfish and flatfish. Some shark fishing is also available here, and the main ocean species have been taken. Worm at low tide. Tackle available locally.

Padstow
Mullet and bass, with some flatfish, right up to the harbour on high tides. The rocks and beaches in the area provide good fishing for bass and pollack, with good

wrasse. Worm plentiful at low tide. Tackle available in Padstow.

Tintagel

Principally rock fishing, with good catches including bass, pollack and bream, and some big conger from Start Point, Tintagel Head, along to Boscastle. The rocks can be dangerous to the inexperienced, and caution is advised, particularly when the sea is rough or backed by a westerly.

Bude

Some of the best south-west bass surf fishing here – Widemouth Bay, Northcott, Crooklets, Sandy Mouth and Summerleaze beaches, also rocks at Dizzard Point. Winter fishing produces mainly whiting, some flatfish and cod. Breakwater at Summerleaze is also rated for bass, with winter flounders at the mouth of the Bude Canal. Bait plentiful at low tide. Tackle available in Bude.

Clovelly

Beach provides bass, conger, pollack, with winter whiting. Boats (from Bideford) in the bay take good catches of reef species and cod in the winter, with the ground off Hartland Point being good for porbeagle shark. Bait fairly easy to find.

Bideford

The harbours and river mouths of this area are excellent fisheries giving bass, big shoals of mullet, and fine stocks of winter flounders, with codling and whiting on the right high tides. The Torridge at Bideford and the river above and below the bridge at Barnstaple are favourite flounder and mullet spots. Appledore harbour also fishes well. Boats are available, giving good offshore fishing, with catches including good rays in latter years. From here, the coast northeastwards begins to be influenced by the Severn mouth and the Bristol Channel, with fewer reef marks. Bass are taken all the way up to Portishead, near Bristol, but rays and winter codling and whiting are more in evidence than they are further west. Bait and tackle available locally.

Ilfracombe

Boats here can offer a variety of fishing, with the main reef and rock species, some sharks, and the tope and rays more associated with the Bristol Channel's shallower waters. The winter codling and whiting fishing can be very good, and the sheltering aspect of the Welsh coast across the Bristol Channel can sometimes allow fishing when the boats of Cornwall are shore-bound by storms. Bait is available locally, but digging worms in the harbour is prohibited during summer. Tackle available locally.

Lynmouth

Good, high tides, especially night tides, are needed to make shore marks fish well, but when the fish are in the shore can be excellent. Bass, with winter codling and whiting and some rays, are taken. The rocks are productive but can be extremely dangerous, especially when backed by a south-westerly. Care must be taken. Bait is fairly plentiful. Boats give access to grounds in the Bristol Channel plus some rock marks, and tope, rays, bass, conger, pollack, coalfish, whiting and flatfish feature among catches. Tackle available locally.

Minehead

A good boat station for Bristol Channel grounds, with catches including bass, conger, tope, rays, flatfish and winter cod and whiting. Of late, small-eyed rays of record size have been taken offshore, and the codling fishing is also improving with

some big fish. The shore is also pro-
ductive in summer and winter, local
favourites being Minehead harbour wall,
Gasworks Beach, Madbrain Beach and
Dunster Beach and the promenade wall.
Boats, tackle and bait available locally.

Watchet
Fishing very much as Minehead (above),
with favourite shore marks being Blue
Anchor, Bridgwater Bay, St Audries Bay,
Doniford, Kilve and East Quantoxhead.
Boats, available locally, give good
catches of bass, angler fish, rays, tope
and winter codling and whiting in Bridgwater Bay. Bait and tackle available
locally.

Weston-super-Mare
Brean Down, Sand Point, Black Rock
and the old pier all fish well for bass,
bream, dogfish, flatfish, thornbacks
(more and more in recent years, from
early spring onwards), silver eels and
winter codling and whiting. In general
this shore needs a good westerly gale and
fishes best on a night high tide. Boats
give access to varied fishing, with some
good rays, plus codling in winter.

Clevedon
Fishing as Weston (above). Bass taken
right up to Portishead, also codling and
whiting on the right tides in winter, with
silver eels generally plentiful. The pier,
which formerly fished extremely well in
winter, is broken and no longer fishable,
but plans are in hand to restore it. Bait
and tackle available locally.

Six

South Wales

Cardiff to St David's Head

The major preoccupations of South Wales sea anglers are bass, tope and, in winter, big cod. The bass fishing west of Swansea, especially around the Gower, is of a high order, while more big tope are taken in Carmarthen Bay (from early May) during a season than in the rest of the British Isles together. Winter cod and whiting are plentiful, and the cod can be big.

A division can be made between the areas influenced by the Severn estuary and those further to the west; Cardiff and the seaside resort of Barry are the dividing line. As with the Somerset and Avon coast, a good high tide backed by a south-westerly generally provides the best sport by taking a good flood of salt water up the river to bring the fish in. This means bass and mullet during the summer, with some rays and dogfish, while winter catches are usually whiting and codling. Without a good tide, catches consist mainly of flounders, some sole and plaice, and silver eels.

Between Cardiff and Swansea the sport in summer improves, and the cod taken in winter are generally bigger. West of Swansea to St David's head, the quality of sport easily matches that of the south-west of England, with an equally varied choice of locations, from rocks, harbours and surf-beaten beaches. Off-shore catches are also good, with plenty of rocky ground to pick up reef species. Shark fishing is also a possibility, although this side of the sport is still being developed.

Harbours and inlets along this coast are invaded in summer by shoals of mullet. Although notoriously difficult to catch, some very big specimens are landed each year. The notable venue for this species is the salt lagoons known as the Leys, to the west of Aberthaw.

Newport
Some bass, flatfish and silver eels, with winter cod and whiting from Goldcliff, St Bride's, Nash and Redwick beaches. Worm from all these areas at low tide. High night tides best for all sport. Tackle available in Newport.

Cardiff
The docks and the foreshore reached through the docks give occasional bass, flatfish, silver eels and winter codling and whiting. Worm can be dug on the foreshore. Tackle shops in Cardiff.

Penarth
Pier and shore fish well for bass, rays, flatfish, silver eels and winter codling and whiting. Bait fairly easily obtainable.

Barry
Boats are available here, giving access to

bass, rays, flatfish and good winter cod and whiting, especially at Jackson's Bay, which also produces tope and dogfish. The shore of Jackson's Bay fishes very well for conger and bass in summer and winter cod. The area near Roose is another local favourite. Barry Docks also give fair catches of all these species. Lug grounds at Watchtower Bay and rag from Sully Island. Tackle available locally.

Porthcawl

Boats available, giving access to Tasker Rocks and Scarweather Sands for rays, dogfish, flatfish, bass and winter codling and whiting. The shore provides good winter fishing, while the pier has yielded several good rays. Lug grounds at Trecco Bay. Tackle available locally.

Swansea

The pier and breakwater at Briton Ferry, Neath shore, Port Talbot and Swansea Docks all provide bass and flatfish, with some rays and winter cod and whiting. Boats are available for fishing in Swansea Bay, especially around the Mumbles and on the Outer Green Grounds. Catches include bass, rays, conger, flatfish, monkfish and codling and whiting. Tackle and bait available locally. Best lug between Oystermouth and West Cross.

Port Eynon

Accessible by the A4118 from Swansea. An ideal base for fishing the Gower, with superb bass fishing and tope, especially around Oxwich Bay, Oxwich Point, and round to Worms Head. Fall Bay is another local favourite for bass, while boats can tackle shoals of bass on Helwick Shoals out to the Helwick Light. Worm grounds are few here, although peeler can be gathered easily. Llanelli is the best bet for worms.

Llanelli

The Burry Inlet is noted for its bass catches, with tope from the shore in many spots. Boats, available locally, give access to the best bass and tope grounds. Worm and crab baits plentiful, with tackle available locally. In winter the Loughor is noted for its flounder catches, with fish to 2 lb and more. Mullet are plentiful in summer but hard to tempt.

Kidwelly

Good bass fishing, especially around the Paula wreck, which is accessible by dinghy. Tope, rays and flatfish also taken from shore marks. Towy and Taf estuaries in the area provide good winter flounder catches. Best worm grounds on the Towy estuary at Ferryside. Tackle available locally.

Tenby

South Beach and Giltar Point are favourite bass spots. Caldy Island (accessible by ferry) provides good rocky ground for spinning for bass, especially at Sandtap Bay and Eel Point. Boats available locally to fish Caldy Sound, Offing Patches off the island, and rock grounds for bass, tope, rays and flatfish. Tackle and bait available locally.

Pembroke

Good shore bass spots at Barafundle Bay and Freshwater East, with mullet in the town's lagoon. Other catches include flatfish and dogfish. Boats, available locally, give access to tope and rays besides bass and flatfish. Tackle and bait available locally.

Milford Haven

The deep water in the haven gives good catches of bass, rays, pollack, conger and flatfish. Mullet are plentiful but hard to tempt. Good shore fishing for bass and flatfish from Chapel Bay, Angle Bay, and Marloes Sands. Boats, available locally, give access to tope and rays besides bass and flatfish. Worm plentiful. Tackle available locally.

St David's
Much of the excellent shore fishing for bass, pollack, tope and flatfish in this area is largely untapped. There are plenty of rocky coves, some difficult to reach but rewarding. Surf bass fishing also at Whitesand Bay. Boats give access to tope, rays, shark and reef species. Bait and tackle available locally, also boat hire and charter.

Seven

West Wales

St David's Head to the Lleyn Peninsula

The principal species of this coast are bass, flatfish and some pollack and mullet in harbours and inlets – a small choice of quarry on the whole, but some good catches are taken, and the scenery is superb. Offshore catches more than make up for this. There are excellent thornback skate, tope and turbot grounds, while shark fishing for blues and porbeagles, still largely in its infancy in the area, is developing fast with some good catches.

The coast, with some exceptions, is rocky and has some excellent spots for spinning or float fishing for bass. Coves give occasional stretches of sand for surf ledgering for bass, and the river mouths attract numbers of mullet and are fine winter spots for flounders. Worm grounds are scarce, and it is perhaps wise always to bring your own if you travel from some well-supplied area to fish this coast. Mackerel are usually plentiful, however; there are limited areas where sandeels can be obtained; and peeler crab is easy to collect among rocks.

Fishguard

A sheltered bay offers bass, pollack, pouting, conger, rays and flatfish, as do the harbour and Fishguard Lower Town. Boats are available, and the offshore fishing for rays, tope, flatfish and dogfish is good. Lug from sandy areas. Tackle available in town.

Cardigan

Surf fishing for bass at Gwbert and Poppit Sands. Flatfish and mackerel also taken here, with rock headlands in the area also offering pollack. Boats are available for fishing out in the bay to the 20-fathom point, where rays and tope are numerous, with some shark. Boats also fish the Teifi estuary for bass. Worm grounds on Poppit Sands. Tackle available in town.

New Quay

Pollack and bass from the headland here, with some flatfish. Spinning from the rocks is the most productive method. The pollack can occasionally be big. Bait limited.

Aberaeron

Bass, mullet, mackerel, pollack, whiting and dogfish from the harbour wall at either side of high tide, with flounders in season. Beaches and rocks north to Aberystwyth, off the A487 coast road, give bass, pollack and flatfish. Bait scarce. Tackle in Aberaeron.

Aberystwyth

Boats available here for fishing out to 20 fathoms. Good mixed catches are taken, including bass, pollack, dogfish, huss, porbeagle and blue sharks, rays, monkfish and black bream. Favourite marks are the Cynfelyn Patches and Sarn Gynfelyn. On the shore, pollack, flounders, whiting and dogfish are taken from the harbour, river mouths and rock areas, with bass off the stone jetty and Tan y Bwlch beach. Mullet plentiful in summer. Some worm can be dug locally. Tackle in Aberystwyth.

Aberdyfi
Ynyslas Dunes on the Dyfi estuary is a good bass mark which also produces flatfish. Shore catches also include rays and dogfish. Boats are available, and most fish the outer edge of the estuary bar for bass, pollack and flatfish. Bait and tackle available locally.

Barmouth
Bass, flatfish and mullet in the Mawddach estuary, favourite spots being the Barmouth rail bridge, the quay, the western end of Ynys y Brawd Island and Penrhyn Point at the estuary mouth. Boats are available to fish sandy grounds to the west of Barmouth for bass, pollack and rays. Some worm on estuary grounds, and mackerel usually plentiful. Tackle in town shops.

Porthmadog
Bass and flatfish mainly in estuary waters, with the favourite spots being the west side of the channel at Morfa Bychan and south bank gullies at Llanfihangel y Traethau. Boats available, giving access to good flatfish grounds in the estuary. Worm grounds near the Glaslyn River. Tackle available in town.

Pwllheli
Bass, mullet and flatfish abound in the harbour area, and Abererch Strand gives good catches of bass and flatfish. Another favourite spot is Gimblet Rock off the promenade. Boats available for bass and flatfish grounds. Tackle shops.

Aberdaron
The sands fish well for bass and flatfish. Boats available for bass, pollack and mackerel fishing off Ynys Gwylan Fawr and Ynys Gwylan Fach islands. Bait limited, although mackerel are usually plentiful. Tackle locally.

Eight

North Wales and Anglesey

The Lleyn Peninsula to the mouth of the Dee

Probably second only to the West Country's superb fishing, the quality of angling along this coast is of a high order. From the coasts, offering a variety of locations from broad, sandy banks to rocky gorges, bass are the main quarry, but there are also flatfish, wrasse, pollack, mullet, and the occasional chance of a shore-caught tope. The cod, notably scarce on the west coast of Wales, reappears here, with some very big fish, especially for winter wreck trips. Offshore tope, big rays, conger, pollack, dogfish and bass all feature in catches. Shark fishing for blues and porbeagles is developing in some places, notably Holyhead. Both spinning and ledgering are popular methods for shore bass and pollack, while the boat marks are usually fished on the drift because of strong tides. Worms are fairly easy to find, and mackerel are usually plentiful.

Nefyn and Trevor

Limited access to the sea, the most popular mark being Trevor quay. Nevertheless long casts can give rewarding catches of bass, flatfish and dogfish. Worm grounds near the quay.

Caernarvon

Quay wall is a local favourite for bass, flounders, mullet and silver eels, with other marks along the Menai Strait at Abermenai Point, Belan Point and Traeth Melynog. There is also a chance of tope from the shore in the Strait. Mullet, bass and flounders in Foryd Creek. Boats available here for tope, bass and flatfish grounds, notably Belan Narrows. Worms from Foryd Creek or Traeth Melynog; tackle available in town.

Port Dinorwic

Bass, mullet, eels and plaice from the Old Quay wall and Moel-y-Don Old Ferry crossing. Winter codling and whiting at the latter mark. Some worm available locally.

Bangor

Bass and plaice, with codling and whiting in winter from the foreshore (pier closed at time of going to press) and sand channels at Traeth Lafan. Boats available for offshore bass grounds. Ragworm from beaches. Tackle in town.

Conwy

Boats available for very good bass fishing over banks and rocks in Conwy Bay, with codling and whiting in season. Good shore fishing, too, from Conwy Morfa to Penmaen Bach, especially for bass and plaice. Worm beds on sands. Tackle in Conwy.

Llandudno

Black Rocks, pier and jetty give bass and

flatfish, with additional conger, wrasse and pollack on the Great Ormes headland. Boats available for grounds outside the Constable Bank, off the headland, which give tope, rays, flatfish, pollack and dogfish. Rag and lug grounds on the west shore. Tackle in Llandudno.

Colwyn Bay
Bass, flatfish and chances of shore-caught tope at Old Colwyn, Rhos-on-Sea, Penrhyn Bay, Tanpenmaen Head, Quarry Jetties, Llanddulas and Kinmel Bay. Victoria Pier is good for bass and flatfish, with some codling in season. Boats available for offshore tope and ray grounds, also monkfish. Lug plentiful and tackle available in town.

Rhyl
Flatfish and some bass in harbour approaches. Boats available for offshore tope, skate and flatfish grounds. Lug on beaches. Tackle in town.

Anglesey

Menai Bridge
Bass, dogfish, pollack, conger, mullet, cod, whiting and wrasse from Britannia Rail Bridge, St George's Pier and slipway, and Ynys Llandysilio island. Boats available for fishing offshore tope, ray, cod, conger and pollack grounds, especially at the Swellies. Rag and lug and tackle available locally.

Beaumaris
Pier, sea wall and Gallows Point are the best local marks for flatfish, bass and some codling and whiting in season. Better catches from boats (available locally). Best worm grounds at Aberlleinog. Tackle available locally.

Amlwch
Boats here for good mixed fishing at Ynys Amlwch, off Bull Bay, Point Lynas sandbanks, and Porth yr Ysgaw, giving catches of skate, rays, cod, pollack, coalfish, congers and whiting. On the shore Point Lynas ledges give catches of the same species, with some bass and dogfish. Local worm grounds and tackle shop.

Holyhead
Breakwater and the British Rail Mail Pier give bass and flatfish, with a chance of conger, rays and tope. Penrhos Beach good for bass, flatfish and mullet, especially in gully area. Boats (available locally) give good sheltered harbour fishing over rocky ground for tope, rays, conger, flatfish, codling and whiting. Good deep-sea fishing up to 10 miles out, with some sharks featuring in catches. Bait and tackle available locally.

Rhosneigr
Bass and flatfish from Rhosneigr rocks and Traeth Crugyll, with chance of rays and tope. Worm grounds at Carreg Goch. Tackle available locally.

Nine

West and North Scotland and the Islands

The Solway Firth to Caithness

It is still true to say that much of Scotland's wealth of sea angling, both boat and shore, is unexplored. Those places which have taken advantage of under-fished grounds are, by and large, favoured by ease of access, and this is also true of fishing in the larger islands. Most also have a strong tradition of commercial fishing providing sound local knowledge.

That said, there is nothing to stop the freelance shore angler, or the angler with a trailed dinghy, exploring out-of-the-way places, especially the larger sea inlets.

Starting with the west coast, the Solway Firth offers flatfish. Wigtown Bay, Luce Bay and Loch Ryan are fast-developing sea fisheries with some fine tope fishing. Rays, conger, dogfish, pollack, haddock, mackerel and cod are also taken.

The complex of inlets around Bute and the Firth of Clyde has a reputation for big cod, besides providing all the species above and some fine flatfish. Gourock is a noted base for the cod grounds of the Gantocks, the Sound of Bute, Wemyss Bay and Loch Long. Cod to 40 lb are taken, although in recent years there are signs that the grounds have been over-exploited because of their popularity, and fresh exploration will give better results. The cod make their way into the Gareloch

at the end of the year, spawn, and leave in early spring (though some fish remain all year). Large areas are sheltered enough for dinghy fishing, and the main fishing methods are jigging with lures or pirks. Feather traces can be effective. Further north is the fine sea-fishing base of Ullapool, noted for catches of big skate, many topping 100 lb, taken both from boats and some shore marks. Again, the coast offers mixed catches, including sharks, hake, tope, monkfish and rays.

On the islands, as on the mainland, the fishing is in various stages of development, and there is little doubt that some great fishing is waiting to be discovered. The angler will be welcomed everywhere, and in places mentioned in this gazetteer where no boat facilities are noted there is always the chance of making local arrangements for a boat trip.

The northern, under-populated coast of Scotland similarly awaits development. Perhaps one of the most attractive prospects besides good mixed catches is the chance of tackling that giant flatfish, the halibut. The Shetlands, the outer islands and the Orkneys offer the same chance.

There are many ports, albeit widely spaced, providing boats in Scotland, some offering the real enthusiast a week at sea rather than day trips. Bait is generally easy to come by, with many worm grounds, shellfish-collecting areas among rocks, and a good supply of the ubiquitous mackerel for boat fishing. Tackle can be obtained in most big centres.

Caulkerbush

Gives access via the A710 from Dumfries to Mersehead Sands. Mainly flatfish, with some rays, dogfish and eels. Rag and lug plentiful locally.

Kippford

Boats are available here for fishing out into the Solway Firth for coalfish, conger, cod, tope, pollack, dogfish, whiting and some rays. Shore fishing from rocks provides all these species. Lugworm obtainable locally. Tackle shop.

Kirkcudbright

Rocks, tidal harbour and wooden jetty give catches of pollack, coalfish, haddock, cod, whiting, conger, dogfish and flatfish. Boats, available locally, give access to good tope grounds in the bay. Local worm grounds and tackle shops.

Isle of Whithorn

Boats here take sharks off Burrow Head in addition to pollack, coalfish, haddock, cod, conger, wrasse and fine tope and dogfish in Wigtown Bay. Rock fishing provides bass in addition to coalfish, pollack, wrasse, conger, codling and whiting. Bait plentiful from local worm grounds. Tackle shops.

Port William

Boats available to fish for tope, flatfish, rays, dogfish and cod in Luce Bay. Shore catches include bass, pollack, coalfish, wrasse, codling and whiting, with some good flatfish. Worm plentiful. Tackle available locally.

Drummore

Another fine centre for the good tope fishing in Luce Bay, with boats for charter or hire locally. Catches also include pollack, coalfish, cod, whiting, rays and dogfish. Main shore species from sands and rocks. Bait fairly easy to find. Tackle locally, but limited, or from Stranraer.

Portpatrick

Good rock fishing in area for coalfish, pollack, cod, conger, haddock and flatfish. Boats available for fishing out into North Channel for mixed bags including rays and skate. Worm beds in harbour.

Stranraer

At the head of the sea loch, Loch Garten, Stranraer offers fine shore fishing for coalfish, pollack, haddock, ling, conger, tope, flatfish and mullet, with codling and whiting in late season. Local favourites include Finnarts Bay, Milluer Point, Lady Bay, Corsewell Point and Port Beg. Boats available for offshore mixed bags, which include common skate, turbot and tope. Worm grounds by Railway Pier; tackle in town.

Girvan

Good rock fishing in area, especially south to Horse Rock, and in the port and from pier. Catches include coalfish, pollack, haddock, flatfish, codling and whiting. Boats available for mixed bags offshore. Tackle in Girvan; worm beds on foreshore.

Ayr

Heads of Ayr, the harbour mouth and Newton shore give dogfish, eels, flatfish, codling and whiting. Flatfish also in Ayr and Doon estuaries. Boats available to fish in the bay for pollack and rays in addition to the above species, with tope grounds around Lady Isle. Worm beds and tackle available locally.

Troon

Several good shore marks extending to Irvine for coalfish, cod, pollack, whiting, dogfish, conger, rays and flatfish. A low tide mark at Barassie gives codling and flatfish. Boats available for mixed catches, including tope. Bait grounds in harbour; tackle in Troon.

Ardrossan and Saltcoats

South Bay, Winton and Montgomery Piers in Ardrossan Harbour, Saltcoats Pier and Stevenson Slag Bing give coalfish, cod, pollack, flatfish and rays. Haddock also taken by boats (available at Saltcoats). Bait plentiful locally. Limited tackle available.

Largs

Entering the Clyde estuary, Largs makes a good base for boat and shore fishing (boats and tackle available locally). Shore marks from Fairlie Flats to Wemyss Bay giving bass, flatfish, cod, haddock, ling, mullet and eels. Boat marks provide tope and the chance of halibut. Worm grounds at Fairlie Flats.

Gourock

Wemyss Pier, Gourock Pier and the shore from Wemyss Bay to Greenock Esplanade give cod, coalfish, conger, haddock, whiting, dogfish and flatfish, with similar mixed catches from boats. Favourite local marks include Ashton Point and Cloche Point. Boats and tackle available locally; worm grounds in Cardwell Bay.

Helensburgh

In the neck of the Gareloch, Helensburgh offers fine shore and boat marks, especially for big cod. Catches also include coalfish, pollack, dogfish, rays, haddock, whiting, flatfish and eels. Boats and tackle are available locally, with worm beds plentiful.

Clynder

A good base for the Rhu Narrows, which provides good cod catches for shore fishermen and additional conger, dogfish and flatfish for boat anglers. Plaice and dabs can be big. Lug and rag grounds locally, with tackle and bait available.

Dunoon

A good base for fishing the Gantocks, Loch Long, Warden's Bank, Hunter's Quay, Skelmorlie Patch and the banks of Inverkip Bay. Large cod are a feature of the area, generally moving in late in the year and staying until spring. Mixed species are also taken by both shore and boat anglers, with some very good plaice from time to time. The pier at Dunoon can also be productive. Tackle, boats and bait available locally.

Oban

Best catches come from Lismore Island and the Firth of Lorne. Cod, pollack, whiting, flatfish and dogfish make up most catches for boats (available locally) and for shore anglers. Tackle and bait available locally.

Mallaig

Like Oban, a noted commercial fishing port. There is fine rock and beach fishing in the area, and the pier can also give good catches, which include codling, haddock, dogfish and flatfish. Additional ling, pollack and skate taken from boats (available locally). Tackle available locally; worms from Morar and Arisaig.

Kyle of Lochalsh

Good mixed catches of all the main species in the harbour and from boats (available locally). Kyle is also the access point for Skye, which offers some fine fishing. Tackle locally; worms from beach.

Shieldaig
Skate often feature in boat catches (boats available locally) out from Shieldaig, and good mixed catches are taken out towards the sea or in the sheltered waters of Loch Torridon. Shore catches include cod, coalfish, pollack, haddock and flatfish. Bait fairly easy to find; tackle limited.

Gairloch
Two big attractions for boat anglers are halibut and common skate, some very big indeed. Ling, pollack, cod, coalfish, haddock, conger, dogfish and flatfish are also taken by boats and shore anglers. Boats, tackle and bait available locally.

Ullapool
Bass, cod, conger, dogfish, flatfish, tope and mullet taken by shore anglers, with Rhu Point and Ardmair Bay being local favourite marks. Ullapool is a fine boat centre, and halibut and big skate feature in catches. Tope, turbot and the species above are also taken. Tackle and bait available locally.

Lochinver
Boats available in Lochinver give access to skate grounds, with cod, pollack, haddock, ling and tope also taken. The harbour, headlands and beaches offer good shore fishing for mixed bags. Tackle and bait available locally.

Thurso
Difficulty of access means that much fine fishing in the extreme north and northwest of Scotland remains untouched, and the enterprising fisherman taking the single-track coast access road will find shore fishing of high quality in abundance. Thurso, served by the A882 trunk road, makes a good base for the area, besides offering some fine fishing on its own account. Beach and rock fishing at Thurso, Holborn Head, Scrabster and Scrabster Harbour and the Old Pier all give cod, ling, pollack, whiting, flatfish and tope. The Pentland Firth and offshore grounds give halibut and skate in addition to the above species and coalfish, conger and angler fish. Bait, tackle and boats available locally.

Keiss
Boats available here for skate, halibut and turbot grounds. Catches also include cod, ling and conger, which are also taken by shore fishermen, with some flatfish. Bait and tackle available locally.

Wick
Boats over Noss Head take extremely good catches of cod, ling, turbot and conger, and there is a very good chance of halibut and big skate. There is every chance, too, of hooking these big fish from the shore in some areas, especially Sinclair's Bay sands. Shellfish bait plentiful; tackle and boats available in Wick.

The Islands

Isle of Arran
Arran undoubtedly offers fishing of a high order, for the most part untouched. The whole area abounds in cod, haddock, coalfish, pollack, ling, conger, flatfish and rays, which may be taken from rocks or boat. Inquire in Brodick for boat chances, especially for Lamlash Bay, which has big skate. Rock marks include Corrie, Sannox and Clauchlands Point. Lug grounds at Brodick and in Lamlash Bay; tackle in Brodick.

Isle of Bute
Rothesay on Bute is a developing sea-angling centre offering boats for cod, pollack, coalfish, conger, rays, dogfish and flatfish. The shore fishing on the island can be excellent, especially in deep water at Garroch Head. Tackle locally, and worms in harbour.

Isles of Coll and Tiree
Fine shore fishing from rocks, with potential never fully explored. The boat fishing has not been developed, but there must be excellent chances of big skate.

Hebrides
As in most of the islands, the potential is enormous; catches from shore and boats and in the many sea lochs are extremely good. Work is being done on developing this potential by the Highlands and Islands Development Board, and the future may see some wonderful grounds opened up, especially for big skate and halibut. Stornoway, on Lewis, offers some boats besides fine local rock fishing. Bait is plentiful. Some tackle in Stornoway.

Isle of Mull
While the greater part of the island offers good shore fishing for all main species, the west coast and Tobermory, plus Calve Island, are the most productive grounds. Skate, pollack, haddock, conger, dogfish and flatfish taken by boats (available in Tobermory). Tackle also in Tobermory, with bait to be found in most parts of the island.

Orkney Islands
Huge skate and halibut are being taken in the waters around the islands, especially Scapa Flow, the Old Man of Hoy, and in the Pentland Firth between the islands and the mainland. Limited boat fishing is available on the islands themselves, but there are boats from Scrabster on the mainland. Boats also take fine catches of cod, ling, pollack, haddock, coalfish, conger and flatfish, all of which may be taken from the shores.

Shetland Islands
Similar high potential as the Orkneys, with halibut taken close to shore in some of the sheltered Voes. Southern Television's angling championships finals used to be fished out from Lerwick on the big, low-freeboard commercial boats, and one which I attended saw some fine catches of ling and haddock (incidentally the match was won by a south coast champion who fished a string of salmon flies to take his ling and haddock). Boats are limited, and inquiries should be made well in advance. Plenty of fish bait available in commercial ports; tackle in Lerwick.

Skye and Raasay
Both islands offer fine shore fishing for mixed catches, Skye also offering boats from Uig and Dunvegan. Catches include cod, coalfish, pollack, haddock, dogfish, conger and the chance of big skate. Tackle in Uig and Dunvegan. Shellfish and worm beds fairly well distributed.

Ten

East Scotland

Wick to Berwick

All of this coast, and especially the northern section, is underdeveloped from a sea-angling point of view and there is much exploration to be done by the adventurous angler. Cod feature largely in catches, with additional coalfish, ling, and the ever-present chance of big skate. Several places offer boat fishing, and the traditional method is drifting with feather traces for cod and cod-related species. From the shore, mussel and shellfish baits take over from worms as the favourite bait, although there are many worm grounds. Bait fishing is generally more productive than spinning.

Lybster
Good fishing both from boats (available locally) and from the shore, with catches including cod, coalfish, haddock, ling, conger, flatfish and skate. Lug at low tide.

Brora
Mixed fishing, as above. Tackle, bait and boats available locally.

Dornoch
The Dornoch Firth can give excellent mixed catches, besides offering sheltered fishing in some storm conditions. Good fishing at Embo from the rocks and pier. Bass and sea-trout also taken from shore, with tope, skate and conger besides cod and flatfish from boats (boat availability limited). Bait and tackle locally.

Cromarty
Boats available here for sheltered Firth waters and offshore grounds, offering good mixed catches including ling, skate, conger and tope. Cromarty, Nigg and Balbair piers are also productive, with occasional bass also taken. Tackle and bait available locally.

Lossiemouth
Beaches offer coalfish, haddock, codling and flatfish, with many sea-trout also taken. Good mixed catches from boats (available locally). West beach and harbour worm grounds. Tackle locally.

Banff
The Deveron estuary, Boyne Bay rocks and the Head of Garness give good shore catches of cod, coalfish, pollack, flatfish, sea-trout, mullet and bass. Harbour and Macduff Pier are also productive. Boats, available locally, return mixed catches of the above species plus sharks, skate and tope. Bait and tackle available locally.

Fraserburgh
Beaches and rocks at Kinnaird Head give good mixed catches. Boats available for good fishing out to sea and in the Moray Firth. Bait and tackle available locally.

Peterhead
Pier, beaches and rocks yield good mixed catches, which include codling, coalfish and flatfish. Additional haddock and ling from boats (available locally). Lug and tackle also available locally.

Aberdeen
Beaches to the north of the town offer good mixed fishing, with cod and flatfish the main species. Coalfish, ling, conger, hake and whiting taken by boats. Boats, bait and tackle available locally.

Stonehaven
Catches here of cod and haddock are very good indeed, with boats in the bay capable of producing big catches. Other species taken are coalfish, hake, pollack and flatfish. Shore anglers take good mixed catches. Worm bait plentiful; boats and tackle available locally.

Montrose
Excellent rock fishing at Scurdie Ness and along the coast to Arbroath. Main catches are cod, coalfish, conger, haddock and flatfish. Pollack, cod, haddock, conger, skate and flatfish taken by boats (available locally). Bait and tackle available.

Arbroath
Harbour and shore give mixed catches, mainly codling and flatfish. Boats are available for grounds giving cod, pollack, coalfish and conger. Worm grounds in harbour. Tackle available.

Tayport
The Tay estuary gives sheltered fishing for codling, coalfish and flatfish. Boats, available locally, also give these species, plus haddock, pollack and conger. Worm grounds in the estuary. Tackle available locally.

St Andrews
Codling, haddock and flatfish from rocks by the harbour. Eden mouth has worm grounds. Tackle in St Andrews.

Anstruther
Boats available here for grounds giving cod, coalfish, ling, haddock and conger. Shore provides mixed catches but mostly codling and flatfish. Beach and harbour provide worms. Tackle available.

Buckhaven
Good mixed catches from the shore, mostly of codling and flatfish. Methil power station outlet, to the north, attracts haddock, cod and whiting, and catches can be big here. Worm grounds on Level beach. Tackle at Methil and Buckhaven.

Burntisland
Harbour walls and breakwater give good catches of codling and coalfish. Boats available for offshore grounds giving mixed catches. Worm grounds on beach. Tackle shop.

Musselburgh
The sea wall is a popular spot for cod, haddock, whiting and flatfish, which are also taken from shore between Cramond and Port Seton. Bait grounds on beach.

North Berwick
Boats available here for good offshore ground for cod, haddock, coalfish, rays and conger. Shore to Dunbar offers good codling fishing. Shellfish grounds along shore. Tackle shop.

Dunbar
Good shore fishing for cod, coalfish,

haddock, whiting and flatfish in the Tyne estuary, Belhaven Beach, The Dells and the harbour. Boats available, which take skate, pollack and conger in addition to the above species. Worms on Belhaven Beach and the estuary. Tackle shop.

Eyemouth
Shore fishes well for codling and flatfish from Burnmouth to Pease. Pollack, coalfish, ling and conger also taken by boats (available locally). Worms from beach and harbour. Tackle shop.

Eleven

Northern Ireland

Londonderry to Warrenpoint

The tourism authorities of Northern and Southern Ireland and their fisheries and agriculture ministries have recognized the worth of sea fishing around the coast as a big draw. However, the angler who requires solitude with the chance of good fish will not be disappointed, for while those places which are now recognized as sea-angling centres do attract many fishermen, there is never the crowding experienced in, say, the South of England or the holiday areas of the South-West. And, as in Scotland, much of the coastal fishing is still unexplored.

Even the state of development of present sea fisheries is limited, with much exploration to be done in such places as the far south-west of Ireland, where there are certain to be grounds containing oceanic sharks and perhaps tunnies.

Underfished grounds, lack of holiday crowds, hospitable people and a wide choice of prospects from harbour fishing to deep-sea charters for big skate all serve to make Ireland as a whole a very good choice for an angling holiday.

Northern Ireland's strands and rocks give fine shore fishing for bass, cod, pollack and flatfish, while boat trips encounter all reef species, with the chance of big tope, skate, and even occasional halibut.

Limavady

A good base for fishing the eastern shore of Lough Foyle and Magilligan Strand to Magilligan Point (take the B202 turn west off the A2 between Coleraine and Limavady). Flounders, small turbot, and big bass from time to time on the strand and in the lough. Local clams, easy to find, are the favourite bait, with worms and peeler crabs fairly easy to collect. Tackle in Londonderry.

Castlerock

The strand at nearby Downhill is over 6 miles long, and principal catches are bass and flounders, with some turbot, usually taken on clam bait, which can be collected locally. It is also easy to reach Magilligan Strand (see Limavady, above). Benone Strand and Castlerock Beach also give bass and flatfish. Tackle shop.

Portrush and Portstewart

Boats available for very good fishing on The Skerries, off Benbane Head, and the Causeway Bank. Year-round fishing for tope, rays, ling, flatfish, cod, haddock and whiting. Shore catches from Portrush East Strand and Portstewart Strand include bass, coalfish, flounders and turbot. Rocks at Ramore Head give additional wrasse, conger, dogfish and pollack. Bann estuary gives flatfish, bass, eels and sea-trout. Bait in the estuary. Tackle shops.

Ballycastle
Boats available for fishing the sound between Ballycastle and Rathlin Island, where occasional porbeagle sharks are taken. Catches also include conger, ling, pollack, coalfish and flatfish. There is also the chance of halibut off Bull Point. Boats also fish Ballingtoy Bay for flatfish, pollack, codling and rays. Flatfish predominate in shore catches from White Park Bay. Bait and tackle available locally.

Carnlough
Good mixed catches taken from boats (available locally), including pollack, coalfish, cod, rays, flatfish and dogfish with some skate. Boat marks off Straidkilly Point and in Red Bay. Shore anglers also take bass. Garron Point, rocks and beaches at Milltown and Waterfoot, Cushendun Strand and headlands all return reasonable catches. Bait can be collected locally.

Larne
Tope, dogfish, pollack and coalfish for boats from Larne off the Maiden Rocks. Muck Island provides good flatfish grounds. Flatfish, pollack and occasional bass from the shore at Brown's Bay. Bait fairly easy to find. Tackle shop.

Carrickfergus
The pier and shore give catches of dogfish, coalfish, codling, whiting and flatfish. Boats, available locally, fish on the drift across Blackhead sandbanks and in Belfast Lough, catches including pollack, coalfish, cod, whiting, haddock, rays and dogfish. Tackle and bait available locally.

Bangor
Local boats fish Belfast Lough for rays, cod and flatfish. Grey Point returns good catches of spurdog, and deeper water produces big hake. Piers and shore give coalfish, codling and whiting. Tackle and bait available locally.

Donaghadee
Boats available here fish the Rigg Bank for cod, dogfish and flatfish. Codling, coalfish, pollack and wrasse from rocks at Orlock Point. Worm beds near harbour and in Sandeel Bay. Tackle shop.

Portavogie
Boats available here to fish for conger, ling, cod and rays off the Ards Peninsula. Pier fishes fairly well for cod, coalfish and some conger eels. Tackle and bait available locally.

Portaferry
Giant skate over the 100-lb mark inhabit Strangford Lough, and Portaferry offers boats to fish for them and tope, spurdogs, huss, rays and conger (all of which can be big). Main boat marks are Skate Rock and Ringhaddy (boats also available at Killyleagh). Flatfish, mullet and sea-trout are taken by shore anglers in the inlets around the lough. Bait and tackle available locally.

Ardglass
Boats available here to fish for pollack, coalfish, cod, rays and flatfish on grounds off Gunn's Island and reefs by Killard Point. Favourite shore marks are the pier and the rocks under the golf course, where pollack, coalfish, big wrasse, dogfish and conger are taken. Worm ground in harbour. Tackle shops.

Newcastle
Cod, pollack, mullet and flatfish in Dundrum Bay for shore and boat anglers (limited boat hire available). Tackle and bait available locally.

Kilkeel
Piers at Kilkeel and Annalong fish fairly well for coalfish, cod, pollack, whiting, dogfish and flatfish. Small coalfish shoal in inner harbour and can be taken on feather traces. Limited boat facilities for grounds which give tope, dogfish, cod and flatfish. Blue shark known to be in region, but fishing for them is not yet developed.

Warrenpoint
Good tope and rays in Carlingford Lough, which also gives mullet, dogfish and conger. Best tackled from boats (available locally). Bass, codling, flatfish and dogfish from the shore at Cranfield Point by the mouth of the lough. Worm grounds and tackle at Warrenpoint.

Twelve

Eastern and Southern Ireland

Dundalk to Bantry Bay

See p. 56 above.

Dundalk
The bay is shallow and the tide takes the water a long way out. The southern end of the bay at Annagassan is the most productive area, giving small bass and flatfish. Bait plentiful.

Clogher Head
Boats from Port Oriel give dogfish, flatfish, whiting and cod. From the shore, the rocks east of the pier on the point of the headland give cod, pollack and coalfish. Some bass from the beach down to Drogheda. Bait plentiful.

Drogheda
Boyne mouth is a good bass mark, and local anglers use peelers and sandeels, which can be collected in the estuary. Another local favourite is Mornington fishmeal factory outlet, which attracts shoals of mullet. Further south at Laytown, bass and flounders are taken where the River Nanny runs across the beach. Sea-trout in tide pool below rail bridge.

Balbriggan
Boats available here to fish for codling, pollack, coalfish, whiting, dogfish and flatfish, especially off Cardy Rocks. Mullet from harbour, and bass and flatfish on the beach to the north where the Devlin River runs across the beach.

Skerries
Boats available for pollack, coalfish, cod, ling, whiting, dogfish and flatfish around the islands, with some very good spurdog, especially between Schenicks Island and St Patrick's Island and Plough Rocks. Outside the islands there is a chance of big tope. Mixed shore species from rocks, sands, and the piers at Loughshinny and Rush. Rogerstown estuary good for bass. Bait plentiful.

Malahide
Broadmeadow Lagoon offers very good mullet fishing (on bread), especially at the Malahide end. Flounders and bass at the outflow and in the estuary. Flounders and occasional bass from rocks at Portmarnock.

Dublin
Boats from Dun Laoghaire, Bulloch Harbour and Bray return catches including pollack, cod, conger, tope and dogfish. Favourite marks are the Muglins, Dalkey Sound, Carrig Rock, Jack's Hole by Dalkey Island (low water), and White Rock (plaice). Bass, pollack, flatfish, dogfish and eels taken from the shore at Howth Pier, Dun Laoghaire piers, Colliemore Pier and Crab Island. Mullet in Dun

Laoghaire and Bullock harbours. Bait grounds on beaches and in harbour areas. Tackle in Dublin.

Bray
Bray piers give pollack, codling, dogfish and some conger eels, with bass and flatfish from the strand below the promenade. Also conger and pollack from rocks at Bray Head, but fishing is dangerous without local knowledge.

Greystones
Boats (available here) take pollack, cod, rays, flatfish, dogfish and tope. Ridge off Red Barn is a favourite mark. Good cod are taken out in the shipping lane, with some big rays. Shingle North Beach can fish well at night for bass, flatfish, tope and some conger eels. The eleven-mile strand between Greystones and Wicklow is reckoned to give some of the best beach fishing on the east coast for occasional bass, pollack, codling, dogfish, tope, rays and flatfish. Lug, rag and mussel bait may be collected at Broad Lough to the north of Wicklow. Tackle in Greystones and Wicklow.

Wicklow
Good flounder fishing in Broad Lough. East pier fishes for pollack, codling, flatfish, rays and congers. Mouth of harbour holds plaice. Silver Strand and Brittas Bay give bass, flatfish and dogfish, with good spurdogs after dark. Good bass and plaice from Redcross River mouth south of Mizen Head. Bait from Broad Lough. Tackle in Wicklow.

Arklow
Rocks and beach to the north of Arklow give catches of bass, codling, flatfish and dogfish. Ferry Bank gives codling and flatfish. Clones Strand gives good chances of shore-caught tope. Steep

beach down to Courtown gives bass, flatfish and dogfish.

Courtown
Beach gives bass and flatfish. Mullet fishing in harbour can be very good. Good bass also at Pollshone Head.

Cahore
Bass and flatfish from pier, rocks and beach, and at Mauricecastle Strand, where there are good chances of shore-caught tope. Good thornbacks and stingray also taken. Bait fairly easy to find.

Blackwater
Bass, flatfish and tope from the shore north of Blackwater at Tinnabearna, with bass and huss from Ballynamona. Bass, tope, dogfish and flatfish from the mouth of the Blackwater, with some angler fish. Bass, tope and flatfish at Blue Pool south of Cush Gap and Curracloe.

Wexford
Boats available here for offshore fishing outside the harbour and on Splaugh Rock, which produces big catches of bass. Rays and flounders are the main catches in the harbour. Tides difficult without local knowledge. Shore fishing in the area and out to Raven Point good for bass and flatfish. Tides need watching while on the sand. Bait plentiful. Tackle in Wexford and Rosslare.

Rosslare
Small boats available from Rosslare Harbour enable anglers to reach the bass shoals over Splaugh Rock in late summer. Again, tide races need watching. Boats also run out to Tusker Rock, which offers mixed catches, including pollack, cod, dogfish, tope and conger. Bass, flatfish and dogfish from the shore from the pier, the cut beside the inner

pier, the beach to Rosslare Point, Black Strand, rocks beyond Greenore Point and St Helens Pier. Mussel and worm baits plentiful. Tackle in Rosslare and Wexford.

Carne
Bass and flatfish from beaches at Carne and Ballytrent, also Carne Pier. Rock outcrop at Carnsore Point also good, with cod, pollack and wrasse in addition to above species. Beach backed by Lady's Island Lake (The Coome) gives bass, flatfish, codling and some tope. Outfall of Tacumshin Lake gives bass, tope and some sea-trout. Small boats available in Carne for offshore bass and tope marks. Bait plentiful.

Kilmore Quay
Spinning for bass from St Patrick's Bridge, a rock outcrop running into the sea near the harbour. Burrow shore gives bass and tope, and Ballyteige Lough offers bass and good flounder fishing. Some limited boat fishing out to Saltee Islands for bass, pollack, conger, tope and rays. Bait fairly easy to find, and fish baits from commercial landings.

Duncannon
Rocky shore from Fethard to Hook Head is good for bass, pollack and wrasse. Fair conger fishing in the small harbour, with bass and flatfish. Boats from Dunmore East, to the west of the harbour entrance, give mixed catches from the harbour and the Race off Hook Head. Further out, there are pollack, conger, dogfish and tope. Shark are known to be in the area but are not yet exploited. Bait and tackle available locally.

Tramore
Bass and flounder can be plentiful on Tramore Strand. The inner bay, Back Strand, dries at low tide, leaving a channel which fishes from either side for bass and flounders. Rock fishing for pollack, wrasse and bass at Brownstown Head and Newtown Head. Worm is plentiful in Back Strand. The area is a popular resort and can be crowded in the day during summer.

Dungarvan
Beaches breaking the cliffs and rocks, at Annestown and Bunmahon, give bass and flatfish. These fish also from Clonea Beach and the Cunnigar sandspit, which cuts off the inner section of Dungarvan Bay. Old rail bridge gives good flounder fishing in winter. Bass inside the sandspit are plentiful from late summer, usually fished from small boats available locally. Sandeel and worm baits can be collected locally. Spring tides best. Dungarvan is a noted deep-sea base, tackling blue shark from July to September. Mine Head gives pollack, coalfish, ling, conger, rays, dogfish and bass. Tackle available locally; also tackle hire.

Ardmore
From Black Rock round Ardmore Bay to Ardmore Head the shore offers good bass and flatfish, especially from Black Rock itself and from the cliffs between the pier and Ardmore Head, and at Ram Head on the southern end of the promontory. Ardmore Strand has lug beds at either end.

Whiting Bay
Between Ardmore and Ferry Point opposite Youghal, the beach is a noted bass area and produced the Irish record fish of 17 lb 1¼ oz in 1977. It also produces flatfish, dogfish and rays, with autumn seeing an influx of painted rays. Rocks at either end of the bay also give bass and flatfish.

Youghal

An excellent boat station for deep-sea and inshore trips, plus some very good shore bass fishing in the Blackwater estuary and surrounding rocks and beaches. Boats from Youghal take blue shark, which move in from mid-June until the end of summer, and skate, rays, cod, pollack, ling, whiting and conger. Small boats in the estuary and grounds just outside the mouth take bass, flatfish, pollack, coalfish and occasional big cod. Mangans Cove, Caliso Bay, Ferry Point, Easter Point, Youghal's piers and jetties, Youghal Strand near the railway station and Pillmore estuary to the south are all good shore marks. Bait plentiful in estuaries. Tackle available in Youghal.

Ballycotton

Formerly one of the premier deep-sea fishing stations in Europe, Ballycotton now has still the fish stocks, but only limited boats for angling. Blue shark, skate, pollack, coalfish, ling, conger and bream feature in catches. The shore fishing is excellent, with bass, pollack, coalfish and flatfish from Ballycotton East Pier, Ballyandreen Bay, Ballycroneen Strand, Ballymona Strand, Garryvoe Beach and rocks at Knockadoon. Lug grounds on Ballymona Strand. Tackle in Ballycotton.

Cobh

Boats and tackle for hire in Cobh and also at Glenbrook and Crosshaven. Boats in the large inland Cork Harbour waters take pollack, codling, conger, skate, rays and flatfish. On offshore grounds blue shark, pollack, ling and conger are taken, with some very big catches indeed. Daunt Rock and wrecks in the area are the main marks. Trabolgan Strand, Inch Strand and Roches Point give tope, bass, wrasse and pollack for shore anglers, with similar fishing and some skate, rays and flatfish at marks within the harbour, such as Monkstown Pier. Worms are plentiful in creeks running into the harbour. Tackle in Cobh, Glenbrook, Crosshaven and Cork.

Kinsale

Kinsale's fame as a boat station has spread far and wide, its reputation based mainly on good catches of blue shark (mid-June to October) and light-tackle fishing for large shoals of big pollack on the Ling Rocks (year-round). Boats also bring in good mixed catches of reef and wreck species and large common skate. Many wrecks are being exploited in the area, especially the *Lusitania* wreck lying in 50 fathoms off Kinsale Old Head. Small boats can be hired to fish in the shelter of Kinsale Harbour for bass, pollack and flatfish. Old and new bridges are other town marks for bass and flatfish for shore fishermen, and there are bass from most beaches and rocks in the area. Worm from harbour shore. Tackle in Kinsale.

Courtmacsherry

Boats and tackle for hire here, giving excellent offshore fishing similar to the chances from Kinsale (above). Kilbrittan Creek and the Arigdeen estuary give mullet, bass and flatfish. Rocks in Courtmacsherry Bay give bass, pollack, dogfish and wrasse. Bait in estuary.

Clonakilty

Good bass and flatfish from Muckruss Strand and the channel behind it to Muckruss Head, also Inchydoney Island at Virgin Mary's Point. Bait and tackle available locally.

Rosscarbery

Fine surf bass fishing from strands in the area, although there are signs that catches are declining, and undersize fish must be returned. Bass, mullet and flat-fish in the lagoon, while outside the estuary mouth pollack are taken from the shore. Lug and sandeels in the estuary. Tackle in Rosscarbery.

Baltimore

The fishing in this south-west finger of Ireland is still largely unexplored, and there is undoubtedly some fine fishing to be found. The boat fishing potential is high, although not yet developed. Lough Hyne, with very deep water close in, gives conger, pollack and wrasse. Boats, which are becoming available in Baltimore, Castletownshead and Schull, are taking pollack, ling, conger, rays and flatfish, plus blue shark, which may be present in large numbers.

Bantry

Boat fishing is limited but developing. Pollack, rays, dogfish, conger and tope are being taken. Offshore reefs and wrecks are not fully exploited and must give good catches, as must shark grounds. Plenty of opportunities for bass, wrasse, pollack and flatfish from the shore. Bait fairly easy to find. Tackle in Bantry.

Thirteen

Western Ireland

Bantry Bay to Donegal

See p. 56 above.

Sneem

Boat fishing is developing here and at Westcove, giving pollack, ling, huss and some skate. Shore fishing is largely unexplored, but many parts offer excellent bass fishing. Bait available locally.

Waterville

On the Kerry tourist ring; the shore fishing is still largely unexplored but some good bass catches are reported from time to time. The shore also produces pollack and wrasse.

Ballinskelligs

Another developing boat station, from which shark grounds may be reached off Lamb's Head. Catches also include huss, pollack, ling and skate. Shore offers bass, wrasse and pollack.

Valentia

A boat station giving access to good shark and skate, plus reef species. Points around the island offer bass, rays, pollack and wrasse. Bait grounds locally.

Glenbeigh

Much of the shore is inaccessible, but where ground can be found, the bass and pollack fishing can be fine. Boats are available at nearby Cromane.

Killorglin

Bass, sea-trout and flatfish from the banks in the Laune estuary from mid-tide up, also from pier. Worm easy to find.

Inch

Inch Strand offers really good storm beach fishing for bass, and also gives flatfish. Rocks to the west of the beach also give bass. Lug grounds at back of sandhills. Annascaul River mouth also good for bass and sea-trout. Spinning is the best approach.

Dingle

A good centre for really fine bass fishing, with pollack, wrasse and flatfish too. Rocky marks at Beenbane Head. Commercial fishing pier attracts shoals of mullet, which can be taken on small baits.

Tralee

Cliffs immediately by the town make fishing impossible, but Tralee is a base for Brandon Bay, where there are ten miles of beaches with really superb bass fishing. Flounders in the Cloghane estuary.

Fenit

A good boat-fishing station for inshore fishing. Catches include common skate, tope, monkfish and big rays. The pier is a noted mark for all these species too, and skate up to 100 lb have been taken. Bass from western side of causeway to Fenit Island. Coastal inlets give bass, flatfish and some very good tope from time to time. Lug from Carrhane Sands, Barrow Harbour and at Fenit. Tackle in Fenit.

Ballybunion

The Cashen River mouth to the south gives bass and flatfish. Bass from beaches and headlands in Ballybunion Bay and at Doon Point and Leck Point to the north. Pollack, wrasse, conger and dogfish also taken from rocks.

Tarbert

A good point for fishing in the Shannon estuary for bass from the ferry pier. Power station hot-water outlet can also be good. Bait easy to find.

Kilrush

On the northern side of the Shannon estuary, Kilrush pier has produced some very good conger. Bass, flatfish, pollack, monkfish and dogfish are also taken. Bait easy to find.

Kilkee

The small bay here, protected by rocks, has produced good bass. Pollack and wrasse are also taken, especially on the rocks to the south.

Doonbeg

Deep water off the rocks at Doonbeg gives good catches of pollack and conger. Porbeagle shark have also been taken. Over the five miles to the north there are four surf beaches giving good catches of bass. Bait fairly easy to find.

Lahinch

The shore here fishes well for bass and flatfish, especially near the mouth of the Inagh River. Cregg Strand can also be good. Lahinch harbour often has shoals of mullet, which can be taken on small pieces of fish. Lug beds east of the harbour and near the Inagh River mouth.

Liscannor

The rocks here have produced big porbeagle shark from July to September. The potential was developed by Jack Shine, a local angler, and his best fish weighed 145 lb. Pollack, wrasse and conger are also taken from the rocks. Cregg has the best bass beach, and there are worm beds here. Boats available.

Doolin

Steep beach giving bass and flatfish, with pollack from rocks at the northern end. Rocks north to Fanore give bass, pollack, wrasse, dogfish and occasional tope.

Fanore

A good surf beach for bass and flatfish. Rocks at southern end give bass, flatfish and some rays. North to Black Head, rocks give bass, pollack, wrasse, conger, dogfish and flatfish.

Ballyvaughan

Boats available here for porbeagle and blue sharks, tope and good catches of main reef species. Tackle may also be hired. Shore in area to Black Head fishes as Fanore (above).

Galway

Principally a boat station, although shoals of mullet invade the harbour and are taken on bread bait. Salthill promenade sometimes gives bass, but is a noted spot for summer mackerel shoals. The boat fishing can be superb, with porbeagle and blue sharks the main quarry. Good catches of reef species are taken year-round.

Spiddal

Another good boat station for Galway Bay fishing, catches including sharks, rays and reef species. Rocky shore gives pollack, wrasse and the occasional bass.

Clifden

Boats from here and nearby Cleggan return catches of sharks, skate and reef fish. In storms, sheltered Mannin Bay gives rays, monkfish and dogfish and occasional big skate. Rocks give pollack, wrasse, some eels and bass.

Westport

Clew Bay's skate fishing is famous, and catches show that many are still present even with heavy fishing in recent years. The big contests here now make sure that all fish caught are returned alive to the water to maintain stocks. Common and white skate are taken, and there is always the chance of shark. Tope, monkfish and reef species are also taken in numbers. There are many shore spots for bass, flat-fish, wrasse and small pollack. Bait and tackle available locally.

Newport

The other main port of Clew Bay, with boats also from Clare Island. Boats can fish out into the open sea for shark be-sides the skate grounds of the bay. Many rocky shore marks for pollack, wrasse and some bass.

Achill Island

Boats available from three harbours on the island – Purteen, Darby's Point, and Bullsmouth. Record Irish blue and por-beagle sharks have been taken off Achill, and there are also good catches of the main reef fish, especially pollack. Rocky shore areas give pollack, wrasse and some bass.

Belmullet

Much of the shore fishing around the peninsula is untried, with plenty of surf stretches and rocks for exploration. Bel-mullet's main importance is as a boat station, and among other records it has produced Ireland's biggest halibut, 156 lb. Fishing out to Black Rock, boats take pollack, ling, cod, bream and tope. Bait and tackle available locally.

Broadhaven

Much of the shore fishing is untried, but boats take good mixed catches around the Erris Race and Eagle Island.

Killala

Boats from here and Enniscrone take blue shark in summer, with fine catches of reef fish and some skate. Small boats concen-trate on the Moy estuary for sea-trout. Bass, pollack, wrasse and flatfish taken from shore and the pier at Enniscrone. Tackle and bait available.

Sligo

Best surf fishing at Strandhill, west of Sligo, for flatfish and some bass. At the neck of Ballisodare Bay, tope are taken from the shore. Small boats in the bay also take tope, which can be plentiful.

Bundoran

Boats here and from Mullaghmore Village take good mixed catches, with pollack and tope the main species. Some blue sharks also taken. Rocks in area give pollack and wrasse.

Ballyshannon

Much of the shore fishing is untried in this area, but there are catches of flatfish and tope, with pollack and conger from rocky areas.

Killybegs

Commercial fishing makes boat hire limited in Killybegs except during angling festivals, when some very good catches indeed are returned. Pollack, coalfish, cod, ling, congers, rays and tope are taken, also some blue shark. Tackle available; fish bait plentiful from commercial landings.

Bunbeg

Boats from here and from nearby Burton-port take pollack, cod, coalfish, haddock and whiting, with rays around Gola. Tope fishing is excellent on some marks. Little shore fishing takes place in the area, but there is no reason to believe it would not be worthwhile.

Rathmullen

Boats available here for fishing the huge tope stocks of Lough Swilly; however, to protect future fishing, catches should be returned alive. Cod, haddock, pollack and whiting taken off Fanad Head, where large spurdogs are also taken. Pollack, coalfish and wrasse from shore rocks at Fanad Head. Worm grounds in Rathmullen Harbour. Tackle available.

Moville

Boats here and from Culdaff and Greencastle for grounds around Malin Head, where some big skate have been taken. Catches also include tope, cod, haddock, whiting, pollack and coalfish. Tope also taken from the main channel in Lough Foyle, with many dogfish. Pollack and coalfish from shore rocks at Dunagree Point. Tackle available.

British Isles Fish Species

Anglers in the British Isles are extremely fortunate in having such a wide range of worthwhile species to fish for; this is due, for the most part, to their unique location between the waters of the North Atlantic warmed by the Gulf Current, and the cold shallow waters of the North Sea.

The species normally keeping to these waters mix to some extent, but an overall picture shows predominant species holding sway for long periods in either summer or winter, moving in or away in spring and early autumn according to whether they favour cold or warm water. This is a simplified picture, for other influences like salinity and choice of breeding grounds also dictate fish movements. However, the movement of cod into the English Channel, particularly eastern regions, in autumn and the influx of black bream from the west, with fewer cod in early summer, fits into the picture; and the same holds true for many species.

All the fish listed below may be expected at some time in British waters. Together with a description of their habitats and an indication of when and where to fish for them, there are suggestions for catching them, based on the experience of many people: local favourite methods and baits are not invariably best, but they are the surest starting-point.

Also given is the British record current at the time this book went to press, and another very good pointer to the size of fish you are likely to encounter in any region – the National Federation of Sea Anglers specimen medal qualifying weights for both boat and shore catches. Comparing your catch with these qualifying weights gives a better picture of how well you have done, for the national record has no reference to the different sizes that members of a particular species reach along different parts of the coast. A list of the areas covered by the weights follows this introduction to species, with a key letter to save much repetition.

Finally, with conservation so much in mind these days, the minimum takeable size (where applicable) is given for the listed species. This is based on ministry minimum sizes deemed necessary to maintain the stocks about the British Isles. That said, though, there is great sense in taking only what you need from the sea and ensuring that surplus catches are always returned without harm to the water.

N F S A Medal Qualifying Weight Regions
A   Cornwall
B   North Devon

C   South Devon
D   Dorset
E   Hampshire and Isle of Wight
F   Sussex
G   Kent, from Sussex border to Margate Stone Pier
H   Suffolk and Norfolk
I   Kent, from Margate, Stone Pier west, and Essex
J   Lincolnshire and Humberside up to Hartlepool
K   Teesside, Tyneside and Northumberland
L   Cumbria, Lancashire and Merseyside
M   Isle of Man
N   Cheshire, Flint, Caernarvon, Denbigh and Anglesey
P   Merioneth, Cardigan
Q   Pembroke, Carmarthen and Glamorgan
R   Avon, Somerset, Monmouth
S   Channel Islands
T   Scotland and Ireland

Angler fish (frogfish):
Lophius piscatorius

A squat, rather ugly fish with a huge mouth and dangling 'bait' hanging from a barbule above the head, the angler fish is common throughout the Atlantic and North Sea and favours muddy or sandy ground, harbours and estuary mouths. It is also found on some rocky ground, especially broken ground with mud and sand patches. It lies on the bottom, often half-submerged in sand or mud. Bottom-living fish, especially small flatfish, and creatures like crabs make up the bulk of its prey, although there have been instances of it rising to the surface to attack sea birds. The angler fish can be very big indeed, and a fish of more than 7 ft long found dead off Kinsale weighed 150 lb. The species undoubtedly gives many breakages to harbour anglers using light tackle for other fish.

Fishing methods
Unless there are grounds where numbers of this fish are known to be present, few anglers set out specifically to fish for angler fish. They have no commercial value, but should be valued for their job as a scavenger and returned to the water. Almost any form of ledgering from shore or boat will take them. Fish baits seem to be favoured.

Season
The bulk of catches is taken in summer, with the fish moving to spawn to deep water during winter and spring.

Record
Boat, 82 lb 12 oz, K. Ponsford, off Mevagissey, 1977; shore, 68 lb 2 oz, H. G. T. Legerton, Canvey Island, 1967.

Medal qualifying weights
Area A, boat 29 lb, shore 18 lb
B, b 25 lb, s 20 lb
C, b 25 lb, s 25 lb
D, b 25 lb, s 20 lb
E, b 25 lb, s 20 lb
F, b 20 lb, s 20 lb
G, b 25 lb, s 20 lb
H, b 20 lb, s 20 lb
I, b 25 lb, s 20 lb
J, b 15 lb, s 15 lb
K, b 15 lb, s 15 lb
L, b 20 lb, s 20 lb
M, b 25 lb, s 15 lb
N, b 20 lb, s 20 lb
P, b 20 lb, s 20 lb
Q, b 20 lb, s 20 lb
R, b 25 lb, s 20 lb
S, b 25 lb, s 20 lb
T, b 25 lb, s 20 lb

Bass
(small fish: **schoolies, chequers**):
Morone labrax

A great favourite with anglers, the bass is a shore and reef fish, and although most are taken in fairly shallow water, its range extends to depths of 100 metres. Fish taken in deep water are often large specimens. A shoal fish, the bass invades harbours and estuaries in the summer months and may extend quite some distance upriver on a high tide. It also comes close in on sandy bays, especially surf beaches, chasing small shoaling fish such as whitebait and sandeels. While the main areas for bass are the South-West, the Channel, the southern North Sea, South and West Wales, Eastern, Southern and West Ireland, they have been taken in many other areas (as the gazetteer entries show). Bass spawn from May to June in British waters.

Fishing methods
A range of approaches can be used to catch bass. In harbours, and from jetties and rocks floatfished or ledgered baits using lightish tackle are useful (line 8 to 12 lb breaking strain), while for surf casters, a bait put out at somewhere near the third breaker will take fish. They sometimes come right in to the beach with a good wave if preoccupied chasing whitebait. On the reefs, bottom-fished baits and drifted baits or lures like rubber sandeels are used. On marks where bass are known to shoal, such as estuary entrances or on the outer fringes of rocks, trolled (trailed) lures, or sandeel or fish strip baits, make for exciting fishing, especially if lightish tackle is used. Spinning can pay off in a variety of locations. Favourite baits are sandeels, peeler crab, ragworm and lugworm, almost any small fish, fish strip, razorfish and other shellfish. While baits to 4 in are usual, some very big bass have been taken (in the Dover area in particular) on ledgered whole herring and mackerel.

Season
In the South-West, the South and West of Ireland, West Wales and even sheltered parts of the Scottish coast, a few bass are taken year-round, but by and large this is a fish of spring, summer and autumn (with the peak of fishing in September). The fish spawns in early summer.

Record
Boat, 18 lb 6 oz, R. G. Slater, off Eddystone Reef, 1975; shore, 18 lb 2 oz, F. C. Borley, Felixstowe, 1943.

Medal qualifying weights
Area A, boat 9 lb, shore 8 lb
B, b 9$\frac{1}{2}$ lb, s 9$\frac{1}{2}$ lb
C, b 9$\frac{1}{2}$ lb, s 9$\frac{1}{2}$ lb
D, b 9$\frac{1}{2}$ lb, s 9$\frac{1}{2}$ lb
E, b 9$\frac{1}{2}$ lb, s 9$\frac{1}{2}$ lb
F, b 10 lb, s 9$\frac{1}{2}$ lb
G, b 9$\frac{1}{2}$ lb, s 9$\frac{1}{2}$ lb
H, b 9$\frac{1}{2}$ lb, s 9$\frac{1}{2}$ lb
I, b 10 lb, s 10 lb
J, b 6 lb, s 6 lb
K, b 6 lb, s 6 lb
L, b 9 lb, s 9 lb
M, b 8 lb, s 7 lb
N, b 9 lb, s 9 lb
P, b 9 lb, s 9 lb
Q, b 9 lb, s 9 lb
R, b 9 lb, s 9 lb
S, b 9 lb, s 9 lb
T, b 10 lb, s 10 lb

Minimum size
15 inches. The bass is a particularly slow grower and stocks face a real threat, so it is important that the size limit should be observed.

Black bream (old wife):
Spondyliasoma cantharas
The arrival of this fish on reef marks off the Channel coast of England, in Western Ireland and parts of the northern North Sea is eagerly awaited. A shoaling fish, deep in the body and marked with characteristic dark vertical bars, it can

provide good fun and some heavy catches on fairly light tackle. On many parts of the coast the fish can be taken from rocky areas of the shore.

Fishing methods
Bream can be taken on feathers, but the normal approach is with a paternoster arrangement of up to four hooks with smallish baits of fish strip or worms. Since the shoals feed above bottom, such a rig is normally lowered right down and then reeled up a few turns when the bottom is hit.

Season
June to October.

Record
Boat, 6 lb 14 oz 4 dr, J. A. Garlick, wreck off South Devon coast, 1977; shore, 4 lb 14 oz 4 dr, R. J. Holloway, Admiralty Pier, Dover, 1977.

Medal qualifying weights
Area A, boat 4 lb, shore 2 lb
B, b 4 lb, s 2 lb
C, b 4½ lb, s 3 lb
D, b 3½ lb, s 2½ lb
E, b 3½ lb, s 2 lb
F, b 4 lb, s 2½ lb
G, b 3½ lb, s 3 lb
H, b 3 lb, s 2 lb
I, b 2 lb, s 1½ lb
J, b 2½ lb, s 2 lb
K, b 2 lb, s 1½ lb
L, b 2½ lb, s 2 lb
M, b 2½ lb, s 1½ lb
N, b 2½ lb, s 2 lb
P, b 2½ lb, s 2 lb
Q, b 2½ lb, s 2 lb
R, b 2½ lb, s 2 lb
S, b 3½ lb, s 2½ lb
T, b 3½ lb, s 2¼ lb

Minimum size
9 inches.

Red bream: *Pagellus bogaraveo*
Like the black bream, a summer visitor. Becomes fairly well distributed but is rather less common in the North Sea. Colour varies from brown through to red and silvery red on its deepish body, with a dark patch on the shoulder behind the upper gill cover.

Fishing methods
As black bream (above).

Season
Throughout summer, with occasional winter fish in south and west.

Record
Boat, 9 lb 8 oz 12 dr, B. H. Reynolds, off Mevagissey, 1974; shore, 4 lb 7 oz, A. Salmon, Alderney, 1980.

Medal qualifying weights
Area A, boat 4 lb, shore 1 lb
B, b 3 lb, s 1 lb
C, b 3¾ lb, s 1 lb
D, b 3½ lb, s 1 lb
E, b 2 lb, s 1 lb
F, b 2 lb, s 1 lb
G, b 2 lb, s 1 lb
H, b 2 lb, s 1 lb
I, b 2 lb, s 1 lb
J, b 2 lb, s 1 lb
K, b 2 lb, s 1 lb
L, b 2 lb, s 1 lb
M, b 2 lb, s 1 lb
N, b 2 lb, s 1 lb
P, b 2 lb, s 1 lb
Q, b 2 lb, s 1 lb
R, b 2 lb, s 1 lb
S, b 3½ lb, s 2½ lb
T, b 3½ lb, s 1 lb

Minimum size
9 inches.

Other breams A few other species of bream visit the coasts of the British Isles but are far less common than the black and red bream. The **bogue** (*Boops boops*) is a rather narrow bream streaked with horizontal stripes. It has prominent notched teeth for browsing on rocks. The **gilt-head** (*Sparus aurata*) is quite rare and has a spectacle-like patch of gold scales linking its eyes. **Pandora's bream** (*Pagellus erythrinus*) resembles the red bream but has larger eyes and no shoulder patch. **Rays bream** (*Brama brama*) is in fact not so closely related to the other breams. It is a deep, silvery fish with sickle-like fins. It is a visitor of warm years, and those trapped when the North Sea becomes cold are often washed up dead.

Records
Bogue: boat, 1 lb 10 oz, D. R. Northam, Plymouth, 1975; shore, 1 lb 15 oz 4 dr, S. Torode, Pembroke, 1978.

Gilt-head: boat, 5 lb, A. Stratton-Knott, St Mawes, 1978; shore, 6 lb 15 oz, H. Solomons, Salcombe, 1977.

Pandora's bream: no record.

Rays bream: boat, 6 lb 3 oz 13 dr, Lt-Col. J. Holland, Barra Head, Scotland, 1978; shore, 7 lb 15 oz 12 dr, G. Walker, Hartlepool, 1967.

Minimum sizes
9 inches all species.

Brill:
Scophthalmus rhombus
This large flatfish favours banks of mud, sand and gravel in shallowish water and is occasionally found in the brackish waters of estuaries. Where these conditions occur, it is fairly widely distributed, like its relative the turbot, with which it is able to hybridize. In general, larger fish are taken in deeper water than the smaller specimens. It can be distinguished from the turbot by having no tubercules (raised spots) on its upper skin, and it has a sharp, forward-pointing

edge to its unbroken fin. Food is sandeels, other small fish and crustaceans.

Fishing methods
Ledgered baits on lines of 10 to 15 lb give best sport. Sandeels, lug and ragworms, fish strip and peeler crab used for bait. Estuarine brill will take baited spoons intended for flounders.

Season
Year-round, with best catches in spring and early summer when fish move into shallow water for breeding. Deep grounds best in winter.

Record
Boat, 16 lb, A. H. Fisher, Isle of Man, 1950; shore, 7 lb 7 oz 8 dr, B. Fletcher, Guernsey, 1980.

Medal qualifying weights
Area A, boat 4½ lb, shore 3¼ lb
B, b 4½ lb, s 3 lb
C, b 6 lb, s 3 lb
D, b 5 lb, s 3 lb
E, b 4½ lb, s 3 lb
F, b 4 lb, s 2 lb
G, b 4½ lb, s 3 lb
H, b 4 lb, s 2½ lb
I, b 4½ lb, s 3 lb
J, b 4 lb, s 2½ lb
K, b 4 lb, s 2½ lb
L, b 4 lb, s 2 lb
M, b 4 lb, s 2½ lb
N, b 4 lb, s 3 lb
P, b 4 lb, s 2 lb
Q, b 4 lb, s 2 lb
R, b 4 lb, s 2 lb
S, b 4 lb, s 2 lb
T, b 5 lb, s 3½ lb

Minimum size
14 inches.

Coalfish (saithe, coley):
Pollachius virens
A dashing relative of the cod, with characteristic dark greeny-brown back

and flanks and a whitish belly. The near-white lateral line cutting along the flank is a good distinguishing mark. Coalfish are fairly well distributed around Britain, with the fry developing in shallow waters and migrating to deeper water as they grow. Spawning is early in the year in deep water. Larger fish found on wrecks and reefs near deep water.

Fishing methods
Coalfish will take a variety of ledgered or drifted baits such as worm, fish strip and peeler crab, and will also go for spinners, lures and jigging pirks, also feathers. Movement in the bait is an attraction. Lines from 15 to 25 lb, more if big fish are known to be present, are recommended. From the shore ledgered or float-fished baits are recommended, the fish favouring rocky ground but sometimes moving into harbours and the like in numbers. Spinning from rocks will also take fish.

Season
Fish taken year-round, with big fish in deep marks in spring.

Record
Boat, 33 lb 7 oz, L. Saunders, off Dartmouth, 1980; shore, 18 lb, B. Hill, Ilfracombe, 1979.

Medal qualifying weights
Area A, boat 17 lb, shore 3½ lb
B, b 14 lb, s 3½ lb
C, b 16½ lb, s 3½ lb
D, b 8 lb, s 2 lb
E, b 5 lb, s 2 lb
F, b 5 lb, s 3 lb
G, b 6 lb, s 3 lb
H, b 6 lb, s 3 lb
I, b 6 lb, s 3 lb
J, b 6 lb, s 3 lb
K, b 6 lb, s 3 lb
L, b 10 lb, s 5 lb
M, b 12 lb, s 9 lb
N, b 10 lb, s 5 lb
P, b 8 lb, s 5 lb
Q, b 8 lb, s 5 lb
R, b 8 lb, s 5 lb
S, b 8 lb, s 5 lb
T, b 10 lb, s 5 lb

Minimum size
12 inches.

Cod (small fish: **codling**):
Gadus morhua
Our most important commercial fish and a favourite with anglers, the cod is present all around the coast, with notable inshore populations during colder weather on the south and east coasts and in the North-West, also north and north-east waters off Ireland. The fish grows big; the boat record is over 50 lb and even the shore-caught record tops 40 lb. Commercial boats take fish above 100 lb. The cod has a fairly catholic taste for the sort of grounds it inhabits but does not approach truly shallow water; fishing from a beach, a deep-water gully will be the best bet.

Fishing methods
Cod will take a variety of ledgered or drifted baits and will also go for spinners, artificial eels, lures and pirks and feather traces. Worm comes top on the list of baits but others are just as effective – peeler crab, mussels and clams (east coast and Northern Ireland), fish and squid strips and sprats. From the shore, casting a ledgered bait to deep water is favoured above other methods. Distance casting plays a good part in successful fishing, unless there are vantage points such as piers and breakwaters to fish from. Strong lines recommended.

Season
Parts of the East and North-East of Britain, north-west Britain and especially parts of western Scotland, the Isle of Man

and Northern Ireland can expect cod year-round, and they do turn up sporadically in summer in almost any area. Nevertheless the greatest numbers appear in these regions, and move down the Channel westwards from the North Sea, from about October onwards, and the colder the winter the more this movement seems to be encouraged.

Record
Boat, 53 lb, G. Martin, Start Point, 1972; shore, 44 lb 8 oz, B. Jones, Barry, 1966.

Medal qualifying weights
Area A, boat 23 lb, shore 9 lb
B, b 18 lb, s 9 lb
C, b 23 lb, s 9 lb
D, b 25 lb, s 15 lb
E, b 28 lb, s 15 lb
F, b 26 lb, s 12 lb
G, b 25 lb, s 19 lb
H, b 23 lb, s 13 lb
I, b 22 lb, s 12 lb
J, b 16 lb, s 16 lb
K, b 16 lb, s 16 lb
L, b 15 lb, s 10 lb
M, b 22 lb, s 10 lb
N, b 15 lb, s 10 lb
P, b 15 lb, s 10 lb
Q, b 15 lb, s 10 lb
R, b 17 lb, s 10 lb
S, b 18 lb, s 12 lb
T, b 22 lb, s 12 lb

Minimum size
12 inches.

Common skate: *Raja batis*
The common skate and the long-nosed skate are the only two species of rays found in British waters that have dark undersides. Although it is likely to turn up almost anywhere in Britain on deep mud, sand or stone grounds, the recognized grounds are off the west coast of Scotland, around the Orkneys, off the Isle of Man and north Wales, and off north, west and south-west Ireland. It grows to more than 300 lb, but the rod-caught record is somewhat less. Feeds on squid, bottom-living fish and crustacea. Capsule-enclosed eggs are laid during spring and summer.

Fishing methods
Because of the strength and large surface area of this big fish, lines of 70-lb breaking strain and up are used, and with the chance of a prolonged fight it is wise to use a harness and butt pad. A wire trace is used to join the line to the hook to avoid the line fraying on the fish's teeth. Simple straight-through ledger rigs are used with baits like whole small fish or a flank of a large mackerel.

Season
Skate can be caught year-round, but most of the boats at the recognized skate-fishing centres put out from June to October.

Record
Boat, 226 lb 8 oz, R. Macpherson, Shetland, 1970. The shore record is open, with a 100-lb minimum qualifying weight. The species is not included in the NFSA medal award scheme.

Minimum size
5 lb, although it is a widespread practice to return all large skates unharmed to the water.

Conger eel: *Conger conger*
The conger is rare in the central and southern North Sea but is fairly widely distributed in other parts of the British Isles, favouring rocky areas and wrecks. A thick-set, powerful fish, it usually has a hole from which it forages for food, afterwards returning to digest its prey, which includes small to medium fish, crabs, lobsters and squid. Many of the

boats in the South-West of England, the best region of Britain for consistently big catches of specimen eels, have reputations based on phenomenal catches. During 1970, a really good year for congers, some giant hauls were made, including several fish over 70 lb, and one of 93 lb (the record was broken twice) by boats working out of the Devon port of Brixham. Since then the 100-lb barrier has been breached at least twice, and the record stands at 109 lb 6 oz.

Fishing methods
While there have been instances of congers taking lures or even feather traces, ledgered baits (whole mackerel or portions of flesh of mackerel, other fish and squid) are the usual approach with lines of 50 lb and up if big eels are expected (70-lb lines are the minimum used on prime marks). On very snaggy ground, breakaway tackle is used, with the main line straight through to a wire trace and hook, and a throwaway weight on weak line attached above the trace. A trapped weight can thus be dealt with by pulling to break the weak line and the rig breaks free. At least one swivel should be incorporated in conger tackle, for once you break a fish clear of its lair it will twist and gyrate all the way to the surface. On less snaggy ground, a simple straight-through ledger rig may be used. Once boated, congers will stay quiet in wet sack. Avoid the powerful jaws and unhook with long-nosed pliers or forceps. If the hook has been gorged, cut the trace rather than trying to retrieve it.

Season
There is a noted migration of congers from inshore waters in cold weather, although a few turn up from time to time in mild winters. Frosts after a late summer can kill numbers of these fish, and one of 158 lb was washed up in such a situation in 1904. The latter part of the summer usually sees the best catches. Conger are thought to spawn only once in life, over grounds between Gibraltar and the Azores during midsummer.

Record
Boat, 109 lb 6 oz, R. W. Potter, Eddystone Reef, 1976; shore, 67 lb 1 oz, A. W. Lander, Torquay, 1967.

Medal qualifying weights
Area A, boat, 48 lb, shore, 20 lb
B, b 40 lb, s 20 lb
C, b 50 lb, s 27 lb
D, b 40 lb, s 30 lb
E, b 30 lb, s 25 lb
F, b 50 lb, s 15 lb
G, b 35 lb, s 20 lb
H, b 25 lb, s 15 lb
I, b 20 lb, s 15 lb
J, b 16 lb, s 16 lb
K, b 16 lb, s 16 lb
L, b 25 lb, s 20 lb
M, b 30 lb, s 25 lb
N, b 25 lb, s 20 lb
P, b 25 lb, s 15 lb
Q, b 25 lb, s 10 lb
R, b 25 lb, s 15 lb
S, b 35 lb, s 25 lb
T, b 35 lb, s 25 lb

Minimum size
28 inches.

Dab: *Limanda limanda*
A small flatfish, the dab favours inshore banks of sand, gravel or mud and may be taken in water less than a foot deep. Fairly well distributed around the British Isles where these conditions occur. Its principal foods are small marine worms and crustacea. Dab fishing with light tackle can be great fun, followed by a tasty fry-up.

Fishing methods
The best approach is a light rig with line

of 5 to 8 lb, a drilled bullet and small hook baited with lug or rag, or pieces of lug or rag, portions of peeler crab or small strips of fish. A light spinning rod, or even a river rod may be used if it is calm with the fishing grounds well sheltered.

Season
Caught year-round, but main catches are in summer. Spawns late winter through to early summer.

Record
Boat, 2 lb 12 oz 4 dr, R. Islip, Gairloch, 1975; shore, 2 lb 9 oz 8 dr, M. L. Watts, Port Talbot, 1936. Not in the NFSA medal award scheme.

Minimum size
8 inches.

Greater spotted dogfish (bull huss, nursehound): *Scyliorhinus stellaris*
The dogfishes and tope are small members of the shark tribe. They are active fish, hunting in packs over broken or weed-patched ground for small fish, crustaceans, worms or squid. Larger on the whole than the lesser spotted dogfish, and not so profusely spotted. Generally found in deeper water than the lesser spotted. Active mainly at night. Widely distributed.

Fishing methods
Ledgered worm or peeler crab, fish strip, squid pieces. On sheltered grounds float-fished baits can be used, held just off bottom. Incorporate wire trace.

Season
Taken year-round, although at the end of summer mature fish migrate to deep water to mate before laying encapsulated eggs.

Record
Boat, 21 lb 3 oz, J. Holmes, Looe, 1955; shore, 17 lb 15 oz, M. Roberts, Falmouth, 1977.

Medal qualifying weights
Area A, boat 14 lb, shore 12 lb
B, b 15 lb, s 12 lb
C, b 15 lb, s 10 lb
D, b 13 lb, s 8 lb
E, b 12 lb, s 8 lb
F, b 14 lb, s 7 lb
G, b 14 lb, s 8 lb
H, b 12 lb, s 6 lb
I, b 10 lb, s 6 lb
J, b 12 lb, s 6 lb
K, b 12 lb, s 6 lb
L, b 13 lb, s 8 lb
M, b 12 lb, s 6 lb
N, b 13 lb, s 8 lb
P, b 14 lb, s 8 lb
Q, b 15 lb, s 8 lb
R, b 14 lb, s 8 lb
S, b 12 lb, s 8 lb
T, b 15 lb, s 12 lb

Minimum size
23 inches.

Lesser spotted dogfish (common dogfish, rough hound): *Scyliorhinus raniculus*
A much smaller fish than the huss, and much more richly spotted. Generally distributed around the British Isles on rough ground, often in quite shallow water. Good to eat when skinned.

Fishing methods
Lighter tackle may be used than for the huss, but the lesser spotted's tastes are similar with a smallish ledgered worm, peeler crab or fish strip bait.

Season
As greater spotted dogfish (above).

Record
Boat, 4 lb 1 oz 13 dr, B. J. Solomon, off Newquay, 1976; shore, 4 lb 8 oz, J. Beattie, Ayr Pier, 1969. Not in the NFSA medal award scheme.

Minimum sizes
Boat, 18 inches; shore, 15 inches.

Spur dogfish (spurdog):
Squalus acanthius
A moderately big dogfish, usually slate grey and occasionally flecked with small star-like white spots. Fairly evenly distributed around the British Isles, with some notable marks producing lots of fish off the east and west coasts of Ireland.

Fishing methods
As other dogfish.

Season
Most fish taken during summer. Gives birth to live young near shores in summer.

Record
Boat, 21 lb 3 oz 7 dr, P. R. Barrett, off Porthleven, 1977; shore, 16 lb 12 oz 8 dr, R. Legg, Chesil Beach, 1964.

Medal qualifying weights
Area A, boat 12 lb, shore 6½ lb
B, b 10 lb, s 8 lb
C, b 10 lb, s 8 lb
D, b 14 lb, s 8 lb
E, b 12 lb, s 8 lb
F, b 15 lb, s 8 lb
G, b 12 lb, s 6 lb
H, b 12 lb, s 8 lb
I, b 10 lb, s 6 lb
J, b 8 lb, s 4 lb
K, b 8 lb, s 4 lb
L, b 12 lb, s 8 lb
M, b 12 lb, s 8 lb
N, b 12 lb, s 8 lb
P, b 10 lb, s 8 lb
Q, b 10 lb, s 8 lb
R, b 10 lb, s 8 lb
S, b 5 lb, s 3 lb
T, b 12½ lb, s 8 lb

Minimum size
23 inches.

Flounder (fluke, butt):
Platichthys flesus
Common all around the British Isles, especially in shallow muddy water and in estuaries, where it will inhabit brackish and even fresh water for some distance upstream. There is a noted influx in these regions during the coldest part of winter as a prelude to moving out to deeper water to spawn. Natural foods are worms and small fish and crustaceans. This fish is often the winter mainstay of shore anglers in many parts of the British Isles.

Fishing methods
Ledgered worm or peeler crab bait on fairly light tackle is the general approach, but flounders may also be taken on small spinners, and a baited spoon (spoon with 2–3-inch hook trace below, baited with worm) is especially good. Other baits are shellfish and small pieces of fish.

Season
Taken year-round, but there is a noted migration into estuaries, creeks and harbours from November through to February. Spawning takes place in early spring.

Record
Boat, 5 lb 11 oz 8 dr, A. G. L. Cobbledick, Fowey, 1956; shore, 5 lb 2 oz, W. Stevens, Teign estuary, 1978.

Medal qualifying weights
Area A, boat 2 lb, shore 2 lb
B, b 2 lb, s 2 lb
C, b 2½ lb, s 2½ lb
D, b 2½ lb, s 2½ lb
E, b 2¼ lb, s 2¼ lb
F, b 2 lb, s 2½ lb
G, b 2½ lb, s 2½ lb
H, b 2 lb, s 2 lb
I, b 2½ lb, s 2 lb
J, b 1¾ lb, s 1¾ lb
K, b 1½ lb, s 1½ lb
L, b 2¼ lb, s 2¼ lb

M, b 1¾ lb, s 1¾ lb
N, b 2¼ lb, s 2¼ lb
P, b 2 lb, s 2 lb
Q, b 2 lb, s 2 lb
R, b 2 lb, s 2 lb
S, b 2 lb, s 2 lb
T, b 2¾ lb, s 2¾ lb

Minimum sizes
Boat, 9 inches; shore, 8 inches, except where otherwise directed by water authorities controlling estuary waters.

Garfish: *Belone belone*
A distinctive green and silver eel-like fish with a long toothed 'beak'. It is often found in association with mackerel, if anything coming rather closer in than the mackerel and taking up residence in sheltered bays and harbours through summer. Natural food is small surface fishes, shrimps and so on. Fun to catch on light tackle. Good to eat if you are not put off by the green bones. Generally distributed, rarer in the North.

Fishing methods
Will take small spinners or mackerel feathers, or small floatfished baits such as tiny pieces of fish or worms.

Season
In parts of the South-West the fish is called 'mackerel guide', for it normally arrives shortly before the main summer shoals of mackerel move in. Spawns near shore in summer. Stays throughout June, July and August.

Record
Boat, 2 lb 13 oz 14 dr, S. Claeskens, off Newton Ferrers, 1971; shore, 2 lb 15 oz 9 dr, M. Wills, The Lizard, 1979.

Medal qualifying weights
Area A, boat 1½ lb, shore 1½ lb
B, b 1½ lb, s 1½ lb
C, b 1½ lb, s 1½ lb

D, b 1¼ lb, s 1¼ lb
E, b 1½ lb, s 1 lb
F, b 1¼ lb, s 1¼ lb
G, b 1¼ lb, s 1 lb
H, b 1¼ lb, s 1 lb
I, b 1¼ lb, s 1¼ lb
J, b 1¾ lb, s 1 lb
K, b 1 lb, s 1 lb
L, b 1 lb, s 1 lb
M, b 1 lb, s 1 lb
N, b 1 lb, s 1 lb
P, b 1½ lb, s 1 lb
Q, b 1½ lb, s 1 lb
R, b 1½ lb, s 1 lb
S, b 2 lb, s 1½ lb
T, b 1¾ lb, s 1¼ lb

Minimum size
15 inches.

Red gurnard: *Aspitrigla cuculus*
This fish is mainly taken in the South and South-West of England and Ireland and in the southern North Sea, but some fish are taken from time to time all around the coast. The gurnards have a characteristic steep forehead, heavily armoured, and 'fingers' or separate rays in front of the pectoral fins, which are large. They grunt quite audibly when boated. More are taken by boat anglers than by shore anglers; they come from a variety of locations but mainly from ground near reefs and wrecks. The red gurnard is good to eat if baked.

Fishing methods
Bottom-fished baits of all kinds are taken – worm, fish strip, peeler crab etc.

Season
Present from spring to autumn in British waters. Spawns in spring and early summer.

Record
Boat, 5 lb, B. Critchley, off Rhyl, 1973; shore, 2 lb 10 oz 11 dr, D. Johns,

Glebe Cove, Cornwall, 1976. Not in the NFSA medal award scheme.

Minimum size
9 inches.

Yellow gurnard (tub gurnard):
Trigla lucerna
A larger gurnard than the red gurnard, with a brilliant blue edge to the pectoral fins which may be faded in older specimens. Body colour is not invariably the colour it gets its name from, and some are muddy brown or blotched. Not an eating fish. Much more widely distributed all around the British Isles than the red gurnard, and many are taken from the shore.

Fishing methods
As red gurnard (above).

Season
As red gurnard, but with occasional winter fish in all areas. Spawns in early summer.

Record
Boat, 11 lb 7 oz 4 dr, C. W. King, Wallasey, 1952; shore, 12 lb 3 oz, G. J. Reynolds, Langland Bay, 1976.

Medal qualifying weights
Area A, boat 5 lb, shore 3¾ lb
B, b 3½ lb, s 2½ lb
C, b 3½ lb, s 2½ lb
D, b 3½ lb, s 2½ lb
E, b 3 lb, s 2 lb
F, b 3½ lb, s 2½ lb
G, b 3½ lb, s 2½ lb
H, b 3 lb, s 2 lb
I, b 2 lb, s 1 lb
J, b 1½ lb, s 1½ lb
K, b 1½ lb, s 1½ lb
L, b 5 lb, s 5 lb
M, b 3 lb, s 3 lb
N, b 5 lb, s 5 lb
P, b 5 lb, s 5 lb
Q, b 5 lb, s 5 lb
R, b 5 lb, s 3 lb
S, b 4 lb, s 3 lb
T, b 5½ lb, s 5½ lb

Minimum size
9 inches.

Other gurnards The **piper** (*Trigla lyra*) is a small gurnard occasionally taken in south-west waters. Similar to the red gurnard, but it has a smooth lateral line, whereas the red gurnard's is ribbed. The **grey gurnard** is another small species and is more widely distributed than the red gurnard. The grey (*Eutrigla gurnardus*) is grey or greyish-red, with whitish spots on the back and flanks. The **streaked gurnard** (*Trigloporus lastoviza*) is an occasional visitor which reaches similar weights to the grey gurnard. Its pectoral fins are reddish, with neat rows of dark blue spots.

Records
Grey gurnard: boat, 2 lb 7 oz, D. Swinbanks, Mull, 1976; shore, 1 lb 8 oz, S. Quine, Peel, 1977.

Streaked gurnard: boat, 12 oz qualifying weight; shore, 1 lb 6 oz 8 dr, H. Livingstone Smith, Clyde, 1971.

Piper record open.

Haddock: *Melanogrammus aeglefinus*
The haddock, a smaller relative of the cod, has a general distribution around the British Isles, but the main concentrations are in northern waters. It shoals over rough ground, where it is taken from midwater down to the bottom, feeding on shoals of smaller fish, squid and crustaceans. An important commercial fish for northern ports. Distinguishable by the silvery appearance and a black blotch on the lateral line behind the pectoral fin, also its tall first dorsal fin. A variant is **Norway haddock** (*Sebastes viviparus*).

Fishing methods
Jigged feathers and lures, also baited hooks, fished on the drift. From shore, paternoster tackle arranged to fish the bait above the bottom.

Season
Caught year-round. Spawns February to May.

Record
Boat, 13 lb 11 oz 4 dr, G. Bones, off Falmouth, 1978; shore, 6 lb 12 oz, G. B. Stevenson, Loch Goil, 1976.

Medal qualifying weights
Area A, boat 9 lb, shore 1 lb
B, b 4 lb, s 1 lb
C, b 5½ lb, s 1 lb
D, b 4 lb, s 1 lb
E, b 4 lb, s 1 lb
F, b 2½ lb, s 1 lb
G, b 3 lb, s 1 lb
H, b 5 lb, s 1 lb
I, b 3 lb, s 1 lb
J, b 4 lb, s 1 lb
K, b 4 lb, s 1 lb
L, b 4 lb, s 1 lb
M, b 6 lb, s 1 lb
N, b 4 lb, s 1 lb
P, b 3 lb, s 1 lb
Q, b 3 lb, s 1 lb
R, b 3 lb, s 1 lb
S, b 3 lb, s 1 lb
T, b 4 lb, s 1 lb

Minimum sizes
Boat, 14 inches; shore, 11 inches.

Hake: *Merluccius merluccius*
A relative of the cod family, slate grey to silvery on the sides and with a dark back. Has none of the barbels associated with other cod family members. Common all around the British Isles, especially the west coasts of Great Britain and Ireland. A deep-water fish; larger specimens are usually taken well offshore.

Fishing methods
Responds to all the methods for haddock (above), but is most likely to be taken on drifted bait just off bottom in deep water.

Season
Comes closest to shore during summer months, moving off to deeper water with the onset of winter. Spawns summer and autumn.

Record
Boat, 25 lb 5 oz 8 dr, H. W. Steele, Belfast Lough, 1962; shore record open, qualifying weight 2 lb 8 oz. Not in the N F S A medal award scheme.

Minimum size
12 inches.

Halibut: *Hippoglossus hippoglossus*
This giant flatfish is most likely to be taken in northern waters, since it shuns warm water. It feeds on bottom-living fishes, crustaceans and molluscs, and occasionally preys on mid-water shoals of fish. More and more anglers are getting bitten by the bug to fish for halibut, travelling to such places as the Shetlands, where they are known to invade the sheltered voes of the coast, the Orkneys, west, north and north-east Scotland, waters north of the Isle of Man and Northern Ireland, and parts of the north-west coast of Ireland.

Fishing methods
Large fish baits, fished on the drift with strong tackle, are the usual method. However, Japanese fishermen who seek halibut in the North Pacific use a scaled-up version of the flounder spoon, a large spoon with a baited hook following, trailed or allowed to play in a strong current.

Season
During winter, especially when a long

period of cold weather sets in. Spawns late winter and early spring.

Record
Boat, 234 lb, C. Booth, off Dunnet Head, 1979; shore record open, qualifying weight 10 lb. Not in the N F S A medal award scheme.

Minimum sizes
Boat, 20 lb; shore, 5 lb.

John Dory (St Peter's fish):
Zeus faber
A deep, flattish fish with a long trailing dorsal fin and a prominent blotch behind the head attributed to St Peter picking the fish up and leaving the mark with his fingers. Common in rocky areas all around Britain, feeding on rock-dwelling crustaceans and small fish.

Fishing methods
Not generally sought out as a species, although it makes fine eating, the fish is most often taken by anglers after other rock fish such as pollack. Smallish worm, fish strip or peeler crab baits give best prospects.

Season
Most fish taken during the summer, which is the main spawning time.

Record
Boat, 11 lb 14 oz, J. Johnson, off New-haven, 1977; shore record open, qualifying weight 3 lb.

Medal qualifying weights
Area A, boat 4½ lb, shore 1 lb
B, b 4½ lb, s 1 lb
C, b 4½ lb, s 1 lb
D, b 4½ lb, s 1 lb
E, b 3 lb, s 1 lb
F, b 3 lb, s 1 lb
G, b 3 lb, s 1 lb
H, b 3 lb, s 1 lb
I, b 3 lb, s 1 lb
J, b 3 lb, s 1 lb
K, b 3 lb, s 1 lb
L, b 3 lb, s 1 lb
M, b 2 lb, s 1 lb
N, b 3 lb, s 1 lb
P, b 3 lb, s 1 lb
Q, b 3 lb, s 1 lb
R, b 3 lb, s 1 lb
S, b 5 lb, s 1 lb
T, b 5 lb, s 1 lb

Minimum size
13 inches.

Lemon sole: *Microstomus kitt*
A smallish flatfish common all around the British Isles, where it lives on shallow sand, gravel and mud banks. Colour is yellow to buff, mottled with darker brown, and the body is rather more elongated than that of the dab, although never so narrow as the common sole. Feeds almost exclusively on worms.

Fishing methods
As for dabs (above). The mouth is adapted to sucking worms from their holes. However, fish are sometimes taken on small pieces of peeler crab or fish strip.

Season
Present year-round, but most fish taken in summer. Spawns throughout summer.

Record
Boat, 2 lb 2 oz, J. Gordon, Loch Long, 1976; shore, 2 lb 7 oz 11 dr, W. Callister, Douglas, 1980. Not in the N F S A medal award scheme.

Minimum size
10 inches.

Ling: *Molva molva*
A long, rather eel-like relative of the cod, with a chin barbel and small barbels near each nostril. A fish of reefs, rocky shores and wrecks, much sought-after by anglers. Common around most of the

British Isles, but can be scarce in the central Channel. Feeds on small fish and rock crustaceans.

Fishing methods
Although ling will take lures, pirks and even feathers, a large fish bait gives the best chance, in preference fished on the bottom near a reef or wreck. Where ground is particularly snaggy, the breakaway tackle described for conger (above) is useful. Ling run quite big (the record exceeds 50 lb), and lines of 25-lb breaking strain and up are recommended.

Season
Taken year-round but sometimes scarce in the North during winter. Best fish come from south-west reefs in late winter and spring, when spawning takes place.

Record
Boat, 57 lb 2 oz 8 dr, H. Solomons, off Mevagissey, 1975; shore, 19 lb 4 oz, D. Rogan, Jersey, 1981.

Medal qualifying weights
Area A, boat 30 lb, shore 4½ lb
B, b 25 lb, s 4½ lb
C, b 30 lb, s 4½ lb
D, b 20 lb, s 5 lb
E, b 10 lb, s 5 lb
F, b 20 lb, s 5 lb
G, b 12 lb, s 5 lb
H, b 12 lb, s 5 lb
I, b 12 lb, s 5 lb
J, b 16 lb, s 5 lb
K, b 16 lb, s 5 lb
L, b 15 lb, s 5 lb
M, b 15 lb, s 5 lb
N, b 15 lb, s 5 lb
P, b 20 lb, s 5 lb
Q, b 20 lb, s 5 lb
R, b 15 lb, s 5 lb
S, b 15 lb, s 3 lb
T, b 25 lb, s 5 lb

Minimum size
28 inches.

Mackerel: *Scomber scombrus*
An important fish commercially and no less so for the angler, to whom the mackerel provides a fine bait and is the reason why many sharks and other fish are drawn into British waters during the summer. It can be taken on jigged feathers when quantities are needed for bait, but it is also fun to take on light tackle.

Fishing methods
As mentioned above, when quantities are needed for bait it is easy to take these fish on jigged feather traces of up to 12 hooks or more. However, it is a dashing fighter and will give fun on a small spinner and 6–8-lb line with a light spinning rod. When shoals are inshore, long-casting with a feather trace or lure will pay off, sweeping the tackle back towards the shore near the surface.

Season
From spring to summer the fish are widely distributed and generally feed near the top on shoals of small surface fish. Later in the year they take to mid-water and bottom feeding. During winter, stocks may disappear from the North Sea if the weather is severe, but there are winter shoals in parts of the Channel and off the South and West of England, Wales and Ireland.

Record
Boat, 5 lb 6 oz 8 dr, S. Beasley, Eddystone, 1969; shore, 4 lb 8 dr, Sqn Ldr P. Porter, Peel, 1952.

Medal qualifying weights
Area A, boat 2 lb, shore 1¾ lb
B, b 1¾ lb, s 1½ lb
C, b 2¼ lb, s 1¾ lb
D, b 1¾ lb, s 1¾ lb
E, b 1¾ lb, s 1¾ lb
F, b 2¼ lb, s 1½ lb
G, b 1¾ lb, s 1½ lb

H, b 1½ lb, s 1½ lb
I, b 1¾ lb, s 1½ lb
J, b 1½ lb, s 1½ lb
K, b 1½ lb, s 1½ lb
L, b 1½ lb, s 1½ lb
M, b 2¼ lb, s 1¾ lb
N, b 2 lb, s 1½ lb
P, b 2 lb, s 1½ lb
Q, b 2 lb, s 1½ lb
R, b 2 lb, s 1¾ lb
S, b 2 lb, s 1¾ lb
T, b 2 lb, s 1¾ lb

Minimum size
12 inches.

Monkfish (angel fish):
Squatina squatina
Widely distributed around the British Isles, favouring muddy grounds, sometimes quite shallow, where they lie half-buried to wait for prey – crustaceans, sandeels and other small fish. A squat, rather ugly, flattened fish, with four characteristic 'wings' on its long, guitar-shaped body.

Fishing methods
Wherever there are known grounds the usual approach is with a ledgered bait, such as a largish piece of fish flesh or a small dab. They run quite large but are of little account as fighters. Lines of 25-lb breaking strain and upwards are recommended.

Season
Taken year-round, but most catches in summer. The fish give birth to 6–25 live young during summer months.

Record
Boat, 66 lb, C. G. Chalk, Shoreham, 1965; shore, 50 lb, R. S. Brown, Monknash Beach, 1974.

Medal qualifying weights
Area A, boat 35 lb, shore 25 lb
B, b 35 lb, s 25 lb

C, b 35 lb, s 25 lb
D, b 35 lb, s 25 lb
E, b 35 lb, s 25 lb
F, b 30 lb, s 25 lb
G, b 35 lb, s 25 lb
H, b 30 lb, s 20 lb
I, b 35 lb, s 25 lb
J, b 15 lb, s 12 lb
K, b 15 lb, s 12 lb
L, b 35 lb, s 25 lb
M, b 25 lb, s 15 lb
N, b 35 lb, s 25 lb
P, b 40 lb, s 25 lb
Q, b 35 lb, s 25 lb
R, b 35 lb, s 25 lb
S, b 35 lb, s 20 lb
T, b 40 lb, s 25 lb

Minimum size
15 lb.

Grey mullet: *Mugil cephalus*
There are three grey mullets that extend to British waters besides the common grey mullet, which is the only mullet with a transparent eyelid. The **thick-lipped grey mullet** (*Crenemugil labrosus*) has a puffy upper lip which is sometimes warty; it is the most common mullet of Irish waters. The **golden grey mullet** (*Liza auratus*) is a smaller species, with a yellowish patch of scales on the head not quite extending to the upper lip. The **thin-lipped grey mullet** (*Mugil capito*) has a similar patch of scales which do extend to the lip, rounded pectoral fins and often a black spot at the base of the pectorals. Mullet are popular shore, harbour and estuary fish, often present in great quantities in summer, although very shy and usually hard to catch. The usual method is float fishing with small hooks, baiting with bread or small scraps of fish, worm or shellfish.

Fishing methods
Floatfished small pieces of bread, fish,

worm or shellfish, or these baits ledgered on paternoster tackle close in to harbour walls, bridge piers etc. While the small-bait approach is generally used, mullet will sometimes take much larger baits intended for other fish. In some circumstances freshwater gear is adequate, but the fish are strong fighters. They also have soft mouths and need careful playing.

Season
By far the biggest concentrations arrive with warm water in the summer, although there are plenty of instances of fish being taken in winter all around the coasts of the British Isles.

Records
There are records for the thick-lipped, thin-lipped and golden grey mullet. Thick-lipped: boat, 10 lb 1 oz, P. C. Libby, Portland, 1952; shore, 14 lb 2 oz 12 dr, R. Gifford, Glamorgan, 1979.

Thin-lipped: boat, 2 lb qualifying weight; shore, 5 lb 11 oz, D. E. Knowles, River Rother, 1975.

Golden grey: boat, 1 lb 14 oz, B. Mercer, Portsmouth Harbour, 1980; shore, 2 lb 10 oz, R. J. Hopkins, Burry Port, nr Llanelli, 1976.

Medal qualifying weights
Area A, boat 3½ lb, shore 4 lb
B, b 4 lb, s 4 lb
C, b 4 lb, s 4 lb
D, b 4 lb, s 4 lb
E, b 4 lb, s 4 lb
F, b 3 lb, s 4 lb
G, b 4 lb, s 4 lb
H, b 4 lb, s 4 lb
I, b 4 lb, s 4 lb
J, b 4 lb, s 4 lb
K, b 4 lb, s 4 lb
L, b 4 lb, s 4 lb
M, b 5 lb, s 5 lb
N, b 4 lb, s 4 lb
P, b 4 lb, s 4 lb
Q, b 4 lb, s 4 lb
R, b 4 lb, s 4 lb
S, b 4 lb, s 4 lb
T, b 5 lb, s 5 lb

Minimum size
13 inches.

Plaice: *Pleuronectes platessa*
A very common flatfish and a great favourite with anglers, besides being of great commercial importance, especially in North Sea fisheries. Favourite grounds are sand and gravel banks, often in quite shallow water, and the fish is known to penetrate estuaries, though not so far as flounders will. Main feed is worms, small crustaceans and molluscs, which it deals with whole by using strong, crushing pharyngeal teeth.

Fishing methods
Ledgered worm, peeler crab or mussel and clam flesh, with best results on light tackle. The species also responds to the flounder spoon method (see under *Flounder* above).

Season
Taken year-round, but migrates to offshore ground in deeper water in winter and spring to spawn.

Record
Boat, 10 lb 3 oz 8 dr, H. Gardiner, Longa Sound, 1974; shore, 8 lb 1 oz 4 dr, N. Mills, Southend Pier, 1976 (both anglers juveniles at times of capture).

Medal qualifying weights
Area A, boat 3½ lb, shore 3¼ lb
B, b 4 lb, s 3¼ lb
C, b 5 lb, s 3½ lb
D, b 4½ lb, s 3¼ lb
E, b 4 lb, s 3 lb
F, b 4 lb, s 3 lb
G, b 4½ lb, s 3 lb
H, b 3¼ lb, s 2½ lb

I, b 3 lb, s 2 lb
J, b 3 lb, s 2 lb
K, b 3 lb, s 2 lb
L, b 3½ lb, s 2½ lb
M, b 4 lb, s 3 lb
N, b 3½ lb, s 2½ lb
P, b 3½ lb, s 2½ lb
Q, b 3½ lb, s 2½ lb
R, b 3½ lb, s 3 lb
S, b 4 lb, s 3½ lb
T, b 5 lb, s 3½ lb

Minimum size
10 inches.

Pollack (lythe): *Pollachius pollachius*

One of the most popular reef and wreck fish, pollack are common off western coasts and on rocky shores and in sea lochs in the north. Although some good specimens are taken from the shore, those from offshore reefs and wrecks are normally much larger. The pollack can have yellow to greenish flanks shading to a dark olive back, and the fish's lateral line appears darker than the flank colour, in contrast to the coalfish's lateral line, which appears white against the flank colour.

Fishing methods

Pollack are hard fighters, accepting worm, squid and fish baits as well as spinners, lures, pirks and feathers. A moving bait drift-fished off the bottom seems to work best. Ledgering with paternoster tackle, spinning and float fishing from rocks will take shore fish.

Season

In most places where pollack are common, specimens will be taken year-round, although the best bet for winter specimens is in south and south-west waters. Younger fish move inshore in spring, stay through summer, and in the autumn migrate to deeper water.

Record

Boat, 25 lb 12 dr, R. Vines, Lyme Bay, 1980; shore, 16 lb, B. Raybould, Portland Bill, 1977.

Medal qualifying weights

Area A, boat 16 lb, shore 6 lb
B, b 16 lb, s 6½ lb
C, b 16¼ lb, s 5 lb
D, b 15 lb, s 6 lb
E, b 12 lb, s 5 lb
F, b 12 lb, s 3 lb
G, b 9 lb, s 5 lb
H, b 9 lb, s 5 lb
I, b 6 lb, s 3 lb
J, b 7 lb, s 7 lb
K, b 7 lb, s 7 lb
L, b 9 lb, s 5 lb
M, b 12 lb, s 7 lb
N, b 9 lb, s 5 lb
P, b 10 lb, s 5 lb
Q, b 10 lb, s 5 lb
R, b 10 lb, s 5 lb
S, b 12 lb, s 6 lb
T, b 12 lb, s 5 lb

Minimum sizes
Boat, 12 inches; shore, 10 inches.

Pouting (pout-whiting, bib):

Trisopterus luscus

Pouting inhabit a variety of localities, greedily attacking any kind of offering, especially those intended for better fish! The fish is a smaller relative of the cod; it has a rather deeper body than other members of the family and, often, four to five darkish vertical bars along the flanks. There is a barbel on the lower lip and a dark spot at the base of the pectoral fins.

Fishing methods

As stated above, pouting will attack all kinds of bait and can be a nuisance. However, if sport is slow and pouting seem the best bet, scale down hook and bait sizes.

Season
The fish are present year-round on deeper marks, moving inshore in numbers in spring and early summer. Main spawning period is March and April.

Record
Boat, 5 lb 8 oz, R. S. Armstrong, off Berry Head, 1969; shore, 3 lb 4 oz, P. Weekes, Dover Breakwater, 1978.

Medal qualifying weights
Area A, boat 3¼ lb, shore 1¼ lb
B, b 3 lb, s 1½ lb
C, b 3¼ lb, s 1½ lb
D, b 3 lb, s 1½ lb
E, b 3 lb, s 2 lb
F, b 3 lb, s 1½ lb
G, b 3¼ lb, s 2½ lb
H, b 2½ lb, s 1½ lb
I, b 2½ lb, s 1½ lb
J, b 2½ lb, s 2 lb
K, b 2½ lb, s 2 lb
L, b 2½ lb, s 2 lb
M, b 3 lb, s 2 lb
N, b 2½ lb, s 2 lb
P, b 2½ lb, s 2 lb
Q, b 2½ lb, s 2 lb
R, b 2½ lb, s 1½ lb
S, b 2¼ lb, s 2 lb
T, b 3 lb, s 1¾ lb

Minimum sizes
Boat, 10 inches; shore, 8 inches.

Thornback ray (roker):
Raja clavata
Our commonest ray, sold commercially as 'skate', the thornback inhabits rough ground or muddy banks. Shoals often consist of fish of a like size and sex; males have pointed teeth, females have flat rounded ones. The grey-to-brown back is mottled with light and dark irregular blotches. There are patches of spines on both wings and in a prominent ridge along the spine and tail.

Fishing methods
Ledgered worms, fish strip, squid or peeler crab.

Season
The thornback breeds on inshore grounds and will sometimes enter river mouths. Females precede the males, arriving in spring from deeper water and staying through summer. Occasional winter fish taken all around the British Isles.

Record
Boat, 38 lb, J. Patterson, Rustington, 1935; shore, 21 lb, R. Brown, Kirkcudbright, 1980.

Medal qualifying weights
Area A, boat 12 lb, shore 9 lb
B, b 11 lb, s 6 lb
C, b 13 lb, s 10 lb
D, b 16 lb, s 10 lb
E, b 15 lb, s 10 lb
F, b 15 lb, s 10 lb
G, b 15 lb, s 11 lb
H, b 18 lb, s 12 lb
I, b 16 lb, s 11 lb
J, b 8 lb, s 5 lb
K, b 8 lb, s 5 lb
L, b 17 lb, s 12 lb
M, b 14 lb, s 12 lb
N, b 17 lb, s 12 lb
P, b 15 lb, s 12 lb
Q, b 14 lb, s 12 lb
R, b 14 lb, s 12 lb
S, b 15 lb, s 12 lb
T, b 15 lb, s 12 lb

Minimum size
5 lb.

Other rays A number of other rays which are similar, in shape at least, to the thornback inhabit British waters. Some are fairly widely distributed and others pretty localized. Care needs to be taken in identifying these fish; their markings provide the best guide. All respond to fishing methods similar to those used for thornbacks (above). The **blonde ray** (*Raja brachyura*) can grow to a good size and is scarce only in the North Sea. It has a brown or sand-coloured disc liberally speckled with darker spots which extend right to the edges of the wings. The **cuckoo ray** (*Raja naevus*) is caught all around Britain but is most common in the south-west and off Ireland. There is a prominent, mottled blotch at the centre of each wing. This is one of the smaller rays. The **sandy ray** (*Raja circularis*) is another small ray, sometimes caught at the western end of the Channel and off Ireland. The disc is covered with smaller spots than those of the blonde ray, and there is a handful of larger, lighter spots towards the centre of each wing. The **small-eyed ray**, or **painted ray** (*Raja microocellata*), is rarely found outside the waters of Devon and Cornwall and off Ireland. There are light and dark circular spots on the back, with short stripes, like brush-marks, running parallel with the margins of the wings. Both the back and underside are spiny. Grows to more than 10 lb. The **spotted ray**, or **homelyn** (*Raja montagui*), is similar to the blonde ray except that the spots stop 2 to 4 cm from the edges of the wings. Occasionally, there is a light circular blotch towards the centre of each wing. Scarce in the North Sea. The **undulate ray** (*Raja undulata*) is rare outside the coastal waters of southern England and southern Ireland. It is a distinctive fish, with an orange or yellow disc marked with dark, wavy stripes like the peel in marmalade. Grows to more than 15 lb.

Records
Blonde ray: boat, 37 lb 12 oz, H. T. Pout,
off Start Point, 1973; shore, 30 lb 4 oz, J. Lowe, Jersey, 1980.

Cuckoo ray: boat, 5 lb 11 oz, V. Morrison, off Causeway Coast, N. Ireland, 1975; shore 4 lb 10 oz, C. Wills, North Cliffs, 1981.

Sandy ray: boat and shore records open, qualifying weight 2 lb.

Small-eyed ray: boat, 16 lb 4 oz, H. T. Pout, Salcombe, 1973; shore, 13 lb 10 oz 3 dr, S. Williams, Camborne, 1979.

Spotted ray: boat, 6 lb 14 oz, H. Jamieson, Causeway Coast, 1978; shore, 8 lb 5 oz, D. Bowen, S. Wales, 1980.

Undulate ray: boat, 19 lb 6 oz 13 dr, L. R. le Page, Herm, 1970; shore, 17 lb 12 oz, K. Skinner, Jersey, 1979.

Medal qualifying weights

Blonde ray:
Area A, boat 25 lb, shore 15 lb
B, b 20 lb, s 5 lb
C, b 20 lb, s 5 lb
D, b 25 lb, s 8 lb
E, b 20 lb, s 8 lb
F, b 15 lb, s 8 lb
G, b 15 lb, s 5 lb
H, b 12 lb, s 5 lb
I, b 12 lb, s 5 lb
J, b 10 lb, s 5 lb
K, b 10 lb, s 5 lb
L, b 15 lb, s 10 lb
M, b 15 lb, s 10 lb
N, b 15 lb, s 10 lb
P, b 15 lb, s 10 lb
Q, b 20 lb, s 10 lb
R, b 20 lb, s 10 lb
S, b 20 lb, s 12 lb
T, b 25 lb, s 20 lb

Small-eyed ray:
A, b 9 lb, s 9 lb
B, b 10 lb, s 8 lb
C, b 11 lb, s 6 lb
D, b 11 lb, s 8 lb

E, b 11 lb, s 10 lb
F, b 12 lb, s 6 lb
G, b 8 lb, s 6 lb
H, b 8 lb, s 5 lb
I, b 8 lb, s 5 lb
J, b 8 lb, s 5 lb
K, b 8 lb, s 5 lb
L, b 8 lb, s 5 lb
M, b 8 lb, s 5 lb
N, b 8 lb, s 5 lb
P, b 8 lb, s 5 lb
Q, b 8 lb, s 5 lb
R, b 8 lb, s 5 lb
S, b 9 lb, s 5 lb
T, b 8 lb, s 5 lb

Spotted ray:
Medal qualifying weight 5½ lb boat or shore, all areas.

Eagle ray:
Myliobatis aquila
The eagle ray, stingray and electric ray belong to different families from the rays above. Both the eagle ray and the sting-ray have venomous tail spines and need careful handling. The fish has wide, tapering wings and a torpedo-shaped body. The tail is thin and whip-like and the spine is near its base. In waters around the British Isles it runs to about 6 lb, and it has been taken in all parts of Britain and Ireland. Occasional very big fish.

Fishing methods
Takes bottom-fished baits of all kinds – worms, fish, squid, peeler crab.

Season
Taken year-round, with noted concentrations off Scottish coasts in winter.

Record
Boat, 52 lb 8 oz, R. J. Smith, off Nab Tower, 1972; shore record open, qualifying weight 15 lb. Not in the NFSA medal award scheme.

Minimum size
3 lb.

Electric ray (crampfish):
Torpedo nobiliana
Common all around the British Isles, where it inhabits shallow banks of sand or mud, lying half-buried in wait for small fish and crustaceans, which it pounces upon and stuns with an electric shock. Has a rounded body with no pro-truding snout and no angular wings found in other rays. Can grow to weights in excess of 50 lb.

Fishing methods
Takes bottom-fished baits of all kinds.

Season
Taken year-round.

Record
Boat, 96 lb 1 oz, N. J. Cowley, off Dodman Point, 1975; shore, 52 lb 11 oz, M. Wills, Porthallow, 1980. Not in the NFSA medal award scheme.

Minimum size
3 lb.

Stingray (fire-flare):
Dasyatis pastinaca
Fairly common all around the British Isles on shallow sandy or muddy banks, where it lies half-buried in wait for crustaceans, molluscs and small fish. Un-like the electric ray it has a pointed snout, straight forward edges to the wings, with rounded tips, and a poisonous spine on the elongated tail. Circe is reputed to have given her son a spear with a sting-ray (trygon) spine, with which he later killed Ulysses.

Fishing methods
Takes bottom-fished baits of all kinds. Where large specimens are expected, heavy tackle is necessary.

Season
Caught year-round, but the main catches are in summer, when the fish sometimes enters estuaries. In summer it gives birth to 6 to 10 live young.

Record
Boat, 61 lb 8 oz, V. Roberts, Cardigan Bay, 1979; shore, 51 lb 4 oz, A. L. Stevens, Sowley Beach, 1975.

Medal qualifying weights
Area A, boat 28 lb, shore 24 lb
B, b 25 lb, s 20 lb
C, b 25 lb, s 20 lb
D, b 25 lb, s 20 lb
E, b 25 lb, s 20 lb
F, b 20 lb, s 20 lb
G, b 25 lb, s 20 lb
H, b 25 lb, s 20 lb
I, b 30 lb, s 25 lb
J, b 10 lb, s 10 lb
K, b 10 lb, s 10 lb
L, b 20 lb, s 15 lb
M, b 20 lb, s 15 lb
N, b 20 lb, s 15 lb
P, b 25 lb, s 20 lb
Q, b 25 lb, s 20 lb
R, b 25 lb, s 15 lb
S, b 25 lb, s 20 lb
T, b 30 lb, s 25 lb

Minimum size
3 lb. However, there is little point in retaining any specimens, and all should be returned to the water unharmed.

Red mullet: *Mullus surmuletus*
Reddish to reddish-brown, with a distinctive sloping forehead and two long, streaming barbels under the lower jaw. It inhabits a variety of grounds, and is caught mainly off the southern and south-western coasts of England and Ireland, and in the North Sea off Scotland. Food consists of crustaceans, molluscs and squid.

Fishing methods
Not normally sought out as a quarry, but likely to be taken on ledgered baits of all kinds.

Season
Main catches in summer. Spawns in summer.

Record
Boat record open, qualifying weight 2 lb; shore, 3 lb 10 oz, J. E. Martel, Guernsey, 1967. Not in the NFSA medal award scheme.

Minimum size
8 inches.

Scad (horse mackerel):
Trachurus trachurus
A silvery, mackerel-shaped fish, but with a prominent row of enlarged scales along the lateral line and very large eyes. It has similar habits to the mackerel and grows to around 2 lb. Rare in the northern North Sea but fairly common elsewhere in the British Isles.

Fishing methods
Not normally sought out as a quarry but responds to the methods listed for mackerel (above).

Season
Summer.

Record
Boat, 3 lb 5 oz 3 dr, M. A. Atkins, Torbay, 1978; shore, 2 lb 15 oz 4 dr, J. Bidgood, Padstow, 1980.

Medal qualifying weights
Area A, boat 1 lb, shore 1 lb
B, b 1 lb, s 1 lb
C, b 1½ lb, s 1¼ lb
D, b 1½ lb, s 1¼ lb
E, b 1½ lb, s 1 lb
F, b 1¼ lb, s 1 lb
G, b 1¼ lb, s 1 lb
H, b 1½ lb, s 1 lb

I, b 1¼ lb, s 1¼ lb
J, b 1½ lb, s 1 lb
K, b 1½ lb, s 1 lb
L, b 1½ lb, s 1 lb
M, b 1 lb, s 1 lb
N, b 1½ lb, s 1 lb
P, b 1 lb, s 1½ lb
Q, b 1½ lb, s 1 lb
R, b 1½ lb, s 1 lb
S, b 1½ lb, s 1 lb
T, b 1½ lb, s 1 lb

Minimum size
8 inches.

Allis shad: *Alosa alosa*

Twaite shad: *Alosa fallax*
Shad are silvery, herring-like fish which penetrate rivers in spring and summer to spawn in fresh water. In the past, many more rivers than at present had runs of these fish, but pollution has had a bad effect. Nevertheless the fish are likely to turn up all around the coasts of Britain and Ireland. The allis shad has a brown smudge on its lateral line directly behind the gill cover, while the twaite shad has up to seven smudges in line along the flank above the lateral line.

Fishing methods
Where there are runs of these fish, as in the lower Severn, they are taken on small fish baits and small spinners.

Season
Caught year-round, but river runs are in spring and early summer.

Records
Allis shad: boat record open, qualifying weight 2 lb; shore, 4 lb 12 oz 7 dr, P. B . Gerrard, Chesil Beach, 1977.
   Twaite shad: boat, 3 lb 2 oz (joint), T. Hayward, Deal, 1949, and S. Jenkins, Torbay, 1954; shore, 2 lb 12 oz, J. W. Martin, Garlieston, 1978.

Medal qualifying weights
Both species:
Area A, boat 1¾ lb, shore 1½ lb
B, b 1½ lb, s 1½ lb
C, b 1½ lb, s 1½ lb
D, b 1½ lb, s 1¼ lb
E, b 1½ lb, s 1¼ lb
F, b 1¼ lb, s 1 lb
G, b 2 lb, s 1½ lb
H, b 1½ lb, s 1½ lb
I, b 2 lb, s 1½ lb
J, b 2 lb, s 1½ lb
K, b 2 lb, s 1½ lb
L, b 1½ lb, s 1½ lb
M, b 1½ lb, s 1¼ lb
N, b 1½ lb, s 1½ lb
P, b 2 lb, s 1½ lb
Q, b 1 lb, s 1 lb
R, b 1 lb, s 1 lb
S, b 1½ lb, s 1¼ lb
T, b 1½ lb, s 1 lb

Minimum size
8 inches.

Blue shark: *Prionace glauca*
Wherever there are large concentrations of mackerel close to deep, oceanic currents, shark are likely to be found – this means that they may be sought for in many more places in the British Isles than at present. Nevertheless, there are now many more centres in north Cornwall, Wales, Ireland, Scotland's west coast and the South of England where boats set out specifically for shark. The blue is one of the smaller sharks, growing to around 150 lb. Before other centres were opened, the recognized place to go for blues was Looe, Cornwall, which is still the base of the Shark Angling Club of Great Britain.

Fishing methods
Fishing methods for all sharks are roughly similar, with a trail of chopped fish bait being laid to lure sharks in range,

when a large mackerel or even a bunch of small ones on a big hook is floatfished. Playing a big shark can be exciting but it is also tiring. Strong tackle is a necessity, and a butt pad and harness ought to be used. Well-equipped shark boats have a belted game chair, able to swivel in any direction, in which the angler is strapped. In limited areas, taken from shore.

Season
Blues arrive with warm water, normally during June in British waters, staying until late summer and moving out when mackerel shoals thin out.

Record
Boat, 218 lb, N. Sutcliffe, Looe, 1959; shore record open, qualifying weight 40 lb.

Medal qualifying weights
Boat only:
Area A, 80 lb
B, 80 lb
C, 80 lb
D, 50 lb
E–R, 40 lb
S, 85 lb
T, 100 lb

Minimum size
40 lb. Again, it is becoming more and more the accepted practice to return all these fish to the water unharmed, in order to preserve stocks. This goes for the other shark species.

Hammerhead shark: *Sphyrna zygaena*
Unmistakable because of the wide, flattened head with eyes at each extremity. Fairly rare in British waters, the hammerhead can reach more than 800 lb.

Fishing methods
As blue shark (above).

Season
Summer visitor.

Not included in British record lists or in the NFSA medal award scheme.

Mako shark: *Isurus oxyrhincus*
A large, strong shark, often leaping clear of the water during fight. The species is sometimes confused with the porbeagle (below). The porbeagle's depth, back to belly, in the region of the pectoral fin, is about a sixth of the total length, while that of the mako in the same region is around one ninth of the length.

Fishing methods
As blue shark (above).

Season
Mainly a summer visitor.

Record
Boat, 500 lb, Mrs J. M. Yallop, off Eddystone, 1971; shore record open, qualifying weight 40 lb.

Medal qualifying weights
Boat only:
Area A, 190 lb
B, 190 lb
C, 190 lb
D, 50 lb
E–S 40 lb
T, 200 lb

Minimum size
40 lb.

Porbeagle shark: *Lamna nasus*
Common all around Britain and Ireland during summer. Grows to around 450 lb.

Fishing methods
As blue shark (above).

Season
Summer visitor.

Record
Boat, 465 lb, J. Potier, off Padstow, 1976; shore record open, qualifying weight 40 lb.

Medal qualifying weights
Boat only:
Area A, 140 lb
B, 140 lb
C, 140 lb
D, 140 lb
E, 140 lb
F, 120 lb
G, 100 lb
H, 50 lb
I, 100 lb
J, 40 lb
K, 40 lb
L, 80 lb
M, 80 lb
N, 80 lb
P, 80 lb
Q, 80 lb
R, 75 lb
S, 175 lb
T, 175 lb

Minimum size
40 lb.

Thresher shark: *Alopias vulpinus*
Distinguishable by the long, tapering upper lobe of the tail fin, which the fish beats on the water to round up and stun shoaling mackerel. Usually found off western coasts but has been caught in the central and eastern Channel.

Fishing methods
As blue shark (above).

Season
Summer and autumn.

Record
Boat, 295 lb, H. Aris, Dunose Head, 1978; shore record open, qualifying weight 40 lb.

Medal qualifying weights
Boat only:
Area A, 110 lb
B, 110 lb
C, 110 lb

D, 110 lb
E, 110 lb
F, 100 lb
G, 80 lb
H, 50 lb
I, 60 lb
J, 40 lb
K, 40 lb
L, 40 lb
M, 40 lb
N, 40 lb
P, 40 lb
Q, 40 lb
R, 40 lb
S, 100 lb
T, 150 lb

Minimum size
40 lb.

Smooth hound: *Mustelus mustelus*
A dogfish growing to around 25 lb, mainly taken in southern and south-western regions over rough ground. Main food is crustaceans, but will take small fish. Grey-skinned, nocturnal.

Fishing methods
Ledgered whole small fish, fish strips, worm or peeler crab.

Season
Most fish taken during summer and autumn.

Record
Boat, 28 lb, A. T. Chilvers, Heacham, 1969; shore, 14 lb 14 oz 12 dr, A. J. Peacock, St Donats, 1977.

Medal qualifying weights
Area A, boat 20 lb, shore 12 lb
B, b 18 lb, s 12 lb
C, b 18 lb, s 12 lb
D, b 15 lb, s 10 lb
E, b 15 lb, s 10 lb
F, b 12 lb, s 15 lb
G, b 14 lb, s 10 lb

H, b 18 lb, s 12 lb
I, b 15 lb, s 10 lb
J, b 12 lb, s 5 lb
K, b 12 lb, s 5 lb
L, b 13 lb, s 10 lb
M, b 15 lb, s 10 lb
N, b 13 lb, s 10 lb
P, b 13 lb, s 10 lb
Q, b 13 lb, s 10 lb
R, b 13 lb, s 10 lb
S, b 5 lb, s 3 lb
T, b 20 lb, s 15 lb

Minimum size
20 inches.

Sole: *Solea solea*

Has an unmistakable elongated, oval shape. Common in the Channel, the North Sea and Irish Sea up as far as Scotland, favouring muddy, shallow banks, where it feeds on small crustaceans, worms and molluscs.

Fishing methods
Small ledgered offerings of worm, mussel or fish flesh on lightish tackle.

Season
Caught year-round.

Record
Boat, 3 lb 12 oz 4 dr, S. Brice, Fishbourn Creek, 1980; shore, 5 lb 7 oz 1 dr, L. Dixon, Alderney, 1980.

Medal qualifying weights
Area A, boat 1¼ lb, shore 1½ lb
B, b 1¾ lb, s 1¾ lb
C, b 1½ lb, s 1¾ lb
D, b 2 lb, s 2 lb
E, b 2 lb, s 2 lb
F, b 2 lb, s 2 lb
G, b 2 lb, s 2 lb
H, b 2 lb, s 2 lb
I, b 2 lb, s 2 lb
J, b 1¾ lb, s 1¾ lb
K, b 1¾ lb, s 1¾ lb
L, b 1½ lb, s 1½ lb
M, b 2 lb, s 2 lb
N, b 1½ lb, s 1½ lb
P, b 1½ lb, s 1½ lb
Q, b 1½ lb, s 1½ lb
R, b 2 lb, s 2 lb
S, b 2 lb, s 2 lb
T, b 1½ lb, s 2 lb

Minimum size
10 inches.

Tope (sweet william):

Galeorhinus galeus
Widely distributed around Britain on shallowish open ground over mud or shingle. Main food is small flatfish. A dashing fighter, much sought-after by anglers.

Fishing methods
Fish bait for preference, but will take worm and peeler, either ledgered on a long flowing trace, or drifted off bottom on suitable ground. Float fishing with the bait held just above bottom is practical in some areas. Lines of 25 lb and up and wire traces recommended.

Season
Most fish taken in summer months but sporadic catches year-round.

Record
Boat, 74 lb 11 oz, A. B. Harries, Caldy Island, 1964; shore, 54 lb 4 oz, D. Hastings, Loch Ryan, 1975.

Medal qualifying weights
Area A, boat 35 lb, shore 35 lb
B, b 40 lb, s 30 lb
C, b 35 lb, s 25 lb
D, b 45 lb, s 30 lb
E, b 35 lb, s 20 lb
F, b 45 lb, s 25 lb
G, b 35 lb, s 20 lb
H, b 35 lb, s 25 lb
I, b 40 lb, s 20 lb

J, b 30 lb, s 15 lb
K, b 30 lb, s 15 lb
L, b 35 lb, s 30 lb
M, b 35 lb, s 30 lb
N, b 35 lb, s 30 lb
P, b 40 lb, s 30 lb
Q, b 40 lb, s 30 lb
R, b 35 lb, s 20 lb
S, b 40 lb, s 30 lb
T, b 45 lb, s 45 lb

Minimum size
20 lb.

Turbot: *Scophthalmus maximus*

A large flatfish which lurks at the edges of sand and gravel banks to ambush sandeels, its main prey, and other small fish. Some good fish also from the fringes of wrecks. Small fish like shallow water and are sometimes found in estuaries. Can grow to more than 25 lb. Skin tubercules distinguish it from brill.

Fishing methods
Ledgered sandeel, fish strip, worms or peeler crab, fished on medium tackle – 15–25-lb breaking-strain line.

Season
Caught year-round, but with heaviest catches in spring and summer. Spawns summer.

Record
Boat, 33 lb 12 oz, R. Simcox, Salcombe, 1980; shore, 28 lb 8 oz, J. D. Dorling, Dunwich Beach, 1973.

Medal qualifying weights
Area A, boat 19 lb, shore 6½ lb
B, b 19 lb, s 7 lb
C, b 19 lb, s 7 lb
D, b 19 lb, s 6½ lb
E, b 15 lb, s 6 lb
F, b 15 lb, s 7 lb
G, b 13 lb, s 7 lb
H, b 12 lb, s 7 lb

I, b 12 lb, s 5 lb
J, b 10 lb, s 7 lb
K, b 10 lb, s 7 lb
L, b 15 lb, s 7 lb
M, b 15 lb, s 5 lb
N, b 15 lb, s 7 lb
P, b 10 lb, s 7 lb
Q, b 10 lb, s 7 lb
R, b 12 lb, s 7 lb
S, b 10 lb, s 6 lb
T, b 19 lb, s 9 lb

Minimum sizes
Boat, 16 inches; shore, 14 inches.

Whiting: *Merlangus merlangus*

A small but commercially important member of the cod family, taken all around the British Isles and in all depths of water, but often coming closer inshore than most species. Has a golden, gently curving lateral line and is silvery in appearance; the colour of the back can range from olive to blue. Feeds on crustaceans and small fish, the latter making up the biggest part of the diet of older fish.

Fishing methods
Often takes bait intended for cod, but scaled-down cod tackle is useful when whiting are predominant. Ledgered baits, either on the bottom or fished above bottom on paternoster tackle, are most effective. While medium tackle is adequate, the chance of cod feeding on the same grounds and in the same conditions means that caution is needed in choice of line breaking strain.

Season
Caught year-round, with bulk of catches in winter.

Record
Boat, 6 lb 12 oz, N. Croft, Falmouth, 1981; shore, 3 lb 7 oz 6 dr, L. Peters, Abbotsbury, Dorset, 1978.

Medal qualifying weights
Area A, boat 3½ lb, shore 1¼ lb
B, b 3 lb, s 1½ lb
C, b 4 lb, s 1¾ lb
D, b 3½ lb, s 1½ lb
E, b 3 lb, s 1½ lb
F, b 3¼ lb, s 1½ lb
G, b 3 lb, s 2 lb
H, b 3½ lb, s 2 lb
I, b 3 lb, s 2 lb
J, b 3½ lb, s 2 lb
K, b 3½ lb, s 2 lb
L, b 3 lb, s 2 lb
M, b 3½ lb, s 2 lb
N, b 3 lb, s 2 lb
P, b 2½ lb, s 1 lb
Q, b 2½ lb, s 2 lb
R, b 2½ lb, s 1½ lb
S, b 2 lb, s 1 lb
T, b 3½ lb, s 2 lb

Minimum sizes
Boat, 12 inches; shore, 11 inches.

Ballan wrasse: *Labrus bergylta*

A very common fish of weedy, rocky areas, found all along the coasts of Britain and Ireland where these conditions occur, and on reefs and wrecks offshore. It browses among the weed fronds for crustaceans, molluscs and tiny fish.

Fishing methods
The best method is to floatfish small offerings of shellfish flesh, peeler crab or fish close to weedy areas. Where practical, paternoster ledgering with these baits is also useful (in harbours, from piers).

Season
Widespread in summer, taken mainly in south-western waters of England and Ireland in winter.

Record
Boat, 7 lb 13 oz 8 dr, D. Gabe, Start Point, 1978; shore, 8 lb 6 oz 6 dr, R. W. le Page, Guernsey, 1976.

Medal qualifying weights
Area A, boat 5 lb, shore 5½ lb
B, b 5 lb, s 5 lb
C, b 5 lb, s 5½ lb
D, b 5 lb, s 5 lb
E, b 3 lb, s 2 lb
F, b 2½ lb, s 3 lb
G, b 2 lb, s 2 lb
H, b 3 lb, s 3 lb
I, b 2 lb, s 2 lb
J, b 3 lb, s 3 lb
K, b 3 lb, s 3 lb
L, b 3 lb, s 3 lb
M, b 4 lb, s 4 lb
N, b 3½ lb, s 3½ lb
P, b 3 lb, s 3 lb
Q, b 3 lb, s 3 lb
R, b 3½ lb, s 3 lb
S, b 5 lb, s 5 lb
T, b 5 lb, s 5 lb

Minimum size
9 inches.

Additional fish species which are either very localized or occasional visitors to British waters are described in *The Penguin Book of Fishing.*

Membership of the National Federation of Sea Anglers is open both to sea-angling clubs and to individual anglers. Details are available from the NFSA Secretary, R. W. Page, 26 Downsview Crescent, Uckfield, Sussex, TN22 1UB. See also p. 107 below.

Tides and Tidal Predictions

Tides are of great importance to sea anglers. Fishing from the shore, the angler wants to know approximately the state of tide for his fishing trip: generally (but not invariably), shore marks fish best on the rising tide, at high water, and for a varying period of the falling tide. This is when fish move in to take advantage of the wealth of food washed from the sand or pebbles of a beach or the weed and crevices of rocks and harbour walls; the falling tide tells them it is time to quit or risk being stranded. For the boat angler, slack water at low and high tide means a chance of anchoring to fish an area that would normally be drifted. On a wreck, for instance, ledger tackle can be sent down for conger and ling during the slack, while it might be better to put down a lure or bait held off the bottom for coalfish or pollack, from a drifting boat, when the tide runs.

Spring and neap tides

Spring tides run up to the highest recorded water level for a particular place on the rise. On the ebb, they run out to the lowest recorded water level (gales can influence this position by either pushing or retarding the surge of water).

Neap tides run up to the lowest recorded high-water level and run out to the highest recorded low-water level.

Between these two extremes are average tides building up to springs or falling away to neaps.

Tidal range

The tidal range is the difference in depth between high water and low water – this is at its greatest on spring tides. The duration of the tide is approximately 6½ hours each way, rise or fall.

Calculating water depth: the Rule of Twelfths

Anglers are able to measure line for a sounding depth with their tackle, but the guide this gives is only rough. Often it is more important to have an accurate assessment of the depth of water, particularly in boat fishing, to avoid becoming trapped on a bank or reef. Another consideration might be making harbour before the water becomes too low to dock. Depths are given on sea charts, but they do not allow for tidal variations, and a simple calculation known as the Rule of Twelfths can be brought into play. (If small inaccuracies are acceptable the duration of the tide can be taken as 6 hours to make the calculation simpler.)

The rule states that the tide rises or falls by:

One twelfth of its range in the first sixth of its duration.

Two twelfths of its range in the second sixth of its duration.

Three twelfths of its range in the third sixth of its duration.

Three twelfths of its range in the fourth sixth of its duration.

Two twelfths of its range in the fifth sixth of its duration.

One twelfth of its range in the last sixth of its duration.

Effect on steep and level beaches

If you take, say, 12 feet of water rising over 6½ hours on a steep beach, its increase over the period would appear gradual. However, if the 12 feet has to fill a shallow bay – and in some instances there is a mile and more between the low- and high-water marks – it can fairly roar in, especially if backed by a wind. This can be dangerous; if there are gullies or depressions in the beach behind the angler, they might fill before he or she has time to reach safe ground. Caution must be observed in such places, and night fishing in particular holds risks – this should never be attempted on a shallow beach with which an angler is unfamiliar.

Tidal streams

The surges of water, or streams, in which the tides around the coast of Britain run follow a set pattern. The maps (Figure 1) show the main stream only at intervals of an hour building up to and falling away from high water (HW) at Dover (streams may in some instances turn into shore an hour before the main stream shown on the map). Figures show the speeds of the streams in knots, the first figure for neaps and the second for springs (approximate only).

Tidal predictions

Anglers living close to the shore are lucky in that local newspapers detail high tide times, and many clubs also give out a local tide timetable. But anglers may wish to plan a trip elsewhere, and the tidal constants in the table below help to find high tide times all around Britain. The times given for a particular area should be added or subtracted from London Bridge high tide times (given in the national press and the main angling newspapers). The data are based on GMT; one hour should be added for British Summer Time. Where first high-water time ('1st HW') is given, the phenomenon known as double high water occurs.

Place	Hours	Minutes
Aberdeen	− 00	20
Aberystwyth	− 06	12
Arbroath	+ 00	26
Arran (Lamlash)	− 01	58
Ayr	− 01	52
Ballycotton	+ 03	43
Banff	− 01	45
Barmouth	− 05	47
Barrow-in-Furness	− 02	23
Belfast	− 02	48
Berwick-upon-Tweed	+ 00	55
Bideford	+ 04	00
Blackpool	− 02	42
Bognor Regis	− 02	38
Boston	+ 04	48
Bournemouth (1st HW)	− 05	08
Bridlington	+ 03	00
Brighton	− 02	52
Bude Haven	+ 03	50
Caernarvon	− 04	02
Cape Wrath	+ 06	05
Cardiff	+ 05	17
Castletown (Bantry Bay)	+ 03	18
Clacton	− 02	11
Cleethorpes	+ 04	07
Cowes (1st HW)	− 02	28
Cromer	+ 05	10

Place	Hours	Minutes
Dartmouth	+ 04	28
Deal	− 02	27
Dornoch		
(Port Mahomack)	− 02	05
Douglas	− 02	41
Dover	− 02	42
Dundee	+ 01	42
Dungeness	− 02	56
Dun Laoghaire	− 01	12
Eastbourne	− 02	52
Exmouth	+ 04	50
Falmouth	+ 03	30
Felixstowe	− 02	15
Filey Bay	+ 02	47
Fishguard	+ 05	38
Folkestone	− 02	55
Fowey	+ 03	48
Gairloch	+ 05	20
Girvan	− 02	05
Gorleston	− 05	01
Hartlepool	+ 01	55
Harwich	− 02	18
Hastings	− 02	47
Herne Bay	− 01	39
Holyhead	− 03	32
Ilfracombe	+ 04	15
Inverness	− 01	40
Irvine	− 01	52
King's Lynn	+ 04	51
Kyle of Lochalsh	+ 05	10
Lamlash: as Arran		
Largs	− 01	42
Leith	+ 00	56
Littlehampton	− 02	38
Llandudno	− 03	02
Londonderry	− 05	41
Looe	+ 03	50
Lossiemouth	− 02	02
Lowestoft	− 04	26
Lyme Regis	+ 04	50
Mablethorpe	+ 04	18
Margate	− 01	50
Menai Bridge	− 03	03
Milford Haven	+ 04	35

Place	Hours	Minutes
Montrose	+ 00	40
Morecambe	− 02	37
Newlyn	+ 03	08
Newquay	+ 03	25
Oban	+ 04	13
Orford Ness	− 02	51
Peel	− 02	41
Penzance	+ 03	08
Peterhead	− 01	00
Plymouth Breakwater	+ 03	54
Porthcawl	+ 04	35
Portland	+ 05	05
Pwllheli Road	− 05	56
Ramsey, IoM	− 02	33
Ramsgate	− 02	22
Rhyl	− 02	58
Rosslare Harbour	+ 04	18
Salcombe	+ 04	05
Scarborough	+ 02	45
Sidmouth	+ 04	50
Skegness	+ 04	30
Southend	− 01	24
Southport	− 02	50
Southsea	− 02	26
South Shields	+ 01	48
Southwold	− 03	51
Spurn Head	+ 03	59
Sunderland	+ 01	48
Swanage (1st HW,		
v. approx. only)	− 05	18
Swansea	+ 04	41
Teignmouth	+ 04	32
Tenby	+ 04	21
Torquay	+ 04	35
Valentia Harbour	+ 02	50
Ventnor	− 02	56
Weston-s-Mare	+ 04	59
Weymouth: as		
Portland		
Whitby	+ 02	19
Whitehaven	− 02	36
Wick	− 02	27
Wigtown Bay	− 02	13
Worthing	− 02	36

Place	Hours	Minutes
Yarmouth, IoW		
(1st HW)	− 03	02
Youghal	+ 03	54

Tidal predictions supplied by the Institute of Oceanographic Sciences (copyright reserved).

Weather and Weather Reports

Wind, fog and rain have a great deal of influence on the angler's comfort and safety, the first two perhaps being of greatest concern for boat fishermen, although fierce rainstorms can restrict visibility severely.

Fortunately we are served by an excellent weather forecasting service, in spite of some highly critical remarks to the contrary. Weather lore is also an asset, and some of the more reliable indicators are given later in this chapter.

Wind The strength of wind influences the size of waves. The best indicator to wind strength remains the Beaufort scale (below). Novice boat fishermen might find conditions becoming uncomfortable at around a fresh breeze, which registers Force 5 on the scale:

0 – Wind less than one knot. Mirror-like surface.
1 – Light air. Wind 1 to 3 knots. Small ripples on surface, no crests.
2 – Light breeze. Wind 4 to 6 knots. Ripples with crests which do not break.
3 – Gentle breeze. Wind 7 to 10 knots. Crests start breaking.
4 – Moderate breeze. Wind 11 to 16 knots. Waves lengthen, with many white horses.

5 – Fresh breeze. Wind 17 to 21 knots. Crested waves with white tops.
6 – Strong breeze. Wind 22 to 27 knots. Large waves with foaming crests.
7 – Moderate gale. Wind 28 to 33 knots. Sea appears to leap, and foam is blown in streaks.
8 – Gale. Wind 34 to 40 knots. Sea rough, with wave crests breaking into flying foam, or spindrift.
9 – Strong gale. Wind 41 to 47 knots. High waves rear up, topple over and roll.
10 – Storm. Wind 48 to 55 knots. Waves very high, and spray begins to affect visibility.
11 – Violent storm. Wind 56 to 63 knots. Waves very high and covered in foam and spray.

Indicators of wind
Barometer rapidly falling or rising. A fall of 6 millibars in a couple of hours (or a rise) can mean a gale follows in 5 to 10 hours. Slower rises and falls more often than not mean less strong winds. Gales which follow a rapid rise in barometric pressure are often squally.

High, thin cloud; mare's tails; mackerel sky. These clouds do not always result in strong winds, but they put you on guard. Should low cloud moving in a different direction to the high cloud appear, and show signs of thickening, a rapid change is about to take place. Low cloud clearing from under high cloud can mean that settled weather is coming in.

Yellow sunset. A bright yellow sky at dusk often precedes wind following a settled period (watery yellow sun usually means rain).

Change of wind direction. A change in wind direction from north, east or south to west or south-west should always be suspected.

Fog Fog is formed when warm, moist air meets cold air or, in the case of sea fog, a cold sea. Sea fog can be very persistent and can be expected at all times but normally in winter between the equinoxes. Winter fogs are normally inshore, where the water is colder than offshore. Summer fogs are normally offshore, inshore water being warmer.

Sea fogs may not clear in winds of Force 6 on the Beaufort scale or less.

Fog, and to some extent rain, sleet and snow, affect visibility and therefore safety. The visibility scale is:

0 – Dense fog. Visibility down to 50 yards or less.
1 – Thick fog. Visibility limited to 300 yards.
2 – Fog. Visibility limited to 600 yards.
3 – Moderate fog. Visibility of half a mile.
4 – Mist or thin fog. Visibility 1 mile.
5 – Poor visibility. 2 miles.
6 – Moderate visibility. 5 miles.
7 – Good visibility. 10 miles.
8 – Very good visibility. 30 miles.
9 – Exceptional visibility. More than 30 miles.

Indicators of fog
Winter: steady high barometer. Anticyclones in winter often create land fogs, and these may widen to sea areas.

Winter: falling barometer following sustained high pressure. This normally means the arrival of warm westerlies which will meet a cold sea. Thus a fog formed might be fairly short-lived unless the barometer steadies and begins to rise again.

Summer: cool northerlies, north-westerlies. Can bring cold air down to mix with warm, moist air. Light winds the biggest risk.

Fog signals given by vessels.
Single foghorn blast repeated every two minutes: Power vessel under way.

Double blast repeated every two minutes: Power vessel under way but not making way.

Long blast and two short blasts, repeated every two minutes: sailing vessel. If under both power and sail, signal as power vessel under way. The same signal is given by vessels not under command, vessels constrained by draught and vessels towing (towed vessel, if manned, gives one long blast followed by three short blasts immediately after the towing vessel's signal).

Rapid ringing of gong or bell for five seconds at intervals of one minute: Vessel at anchor.

Rapid ringing of gong or bell with three distinct strokes of gong or bell in interval: Vessel aground.

Vessels of 100 metres or more also sound gong aft following fog signal.

It is important that small fishing boats carry a handbell or horn for use in fog. A compass is also essential.

Rain The rapid changes of barometric pressure which precede wind also foretell rain, more especially with a rapidly falling barometer.

Other indicators of rain
Watery yellow sunset, sun appearing pale, luminous rings round moon. These mean that high clouds of ice particles are moving in, usually in advance of a depression.

High sunset. That is, a sunset which comes early through clouds massing above the horizon (especially apparently unbroken cloud). This means that the cloud cover lies a considerable distance to the west. Conversely, if the sun has set and continues to illuminate clouds on the horizon, the sky west of the cloud must be clear and fine weather is therefore following.

Good weather A settled barometer indicates settled weather, especially a settled high pressure (but in autumn, winter and spring this may lead to fog, either localized or widespread).

Other indicators of good weather
Pink sunset. Red sky at night etc., etc. A reasonable indicator of fine weather.

Small, fleecy clouds. These are usually present through spells of fine weather.

Light easterlies. This quarter of the wind indicates that an anti-cyclone holds sway.

Meteorological offices

North-East Scotland:	Kirkwall Airport, Orkney. Tel. Kirkwall (0856) 2421, ext. 34. Aberdeen Airport. Tel. Aberdeen (0224) 722334. Kinloss. Tel. Forres (0309) 2161, ext. 673/674.
Eastern Scotland:	Pitreavie. Tel. Inverkeithing (038 34) 2566.
North-East	Newcastle Weather Centre.
England:	Tel. Newcastle (0632) 26453.
North-West England:	Manchester Weather Centre. Tel. Manchester (061) 832 6701.
Eastern England:	Bawtry, S Yorks. Tel. Doncaster (0302) 710474. Honington, Suffolk. Tel. Honington (035 96) 466.
Midlands:	Nottingham Weather Centre. Tel. Nottingham (0602) 384092.
South-East England:	London Weather Centre. Tel. (01) 836 4311.
Southern England:	Southampton Weather Centre. Tel. Southampton (0703) 28844.
South-West England:	Plymouth. Tel. Plymouth (0752) 42534.
Western England:	Gloucester. Tel. Churchdown (0452) 855566.
South Wales:	As Western England (Gloucester) above.
North Wales:	As North-West England (Manchester) above. Also Valley, Gwynedd. Tel. Holyhead (0407) 2288.
West Scotland:	Glasgow Weather Centre. Tel. Glasgow (041) 248 3451.
Northern Ireland:	Belfast (Aldergrove) Airport. Tel. Crumlin (084 94) 52339.

BBC Radio Shipping Forecasts (see Figure 2), Radio 4, 1500m/200 KHz daily at 0015, 0625, 1355, and 1750.

Inshore waters forecast at end of Radio 4 programmes every day and on Radio 3, 247 m/1215 KHz weekdays at 0655 and Saturday and Sunday at 0755.

BBC Radio Weather Forecasts

Time	Station	Contents
0010 daily	4	General forecast and summary
0604 M–Fri.	4	General forecast
0617 M–Fri.	2	Farming forecast
0635 Sat.	R. Wales	Welsh weather
0640 Sat.	4	Farming
0655 M–Sat.	4	General forecast
0655 M–Fri.	3	UK general, plus inshore waters
0702 S–Sun.	1 and 2	General forecast
0704 M–Fri.	R. London	London area
0740 M–Sat.	R. Wales	Welsh weather
0755 daily	4	General forecast
0755 S–Sun.	3	UK general, plus inshore waters
0755 Sun.	R. Wales	UK general, Wales in detail
0802 S–Sun.	2	General forecast
0804 daily	R. London	London area
0843 Sat.	4	Sporting events plus weather summary
0855 Sun.	4	General forecast
0855 Sun.	R. Wales	UK general, Wales in detail
1020 Sat.	2	General
1255 daily	4	General
1255 M–Fri.	R. Wales	UK general, Wales in detail
1755 daily	4	General forecast
1755 M–Fri.	R. Wales	UK general, Wales in detail
1802 Sat.	2	General forecast
1832 M–Fri.	2	General forecast

Telephone Recorded Weather Reports

Anglesey and North Wales coast	(061 246) 8093
Bedford area (40-mile radius)	(0582) 8091
Birmingham and Warwickshire	(021 246) 8091
Devon and Cornwall	(0752) 8091
Dorset and Hants coast	(0703) 8091
East Midlands	(0602) 8091
Edinburgh and Lothian	(031 246) 8091
Essex coast	(01 246) 8096
Glamorgan and Gwent	(0222) 8091
Glasgow area	(041 246) 8091
Kent coast	(01 246) 8098
Lincs and Humberside	(0522) 8091
London area	(0483) 8091
Norfolk and Suffolk	(0473) 8091
North-East England incl. North Yorks	(0632) 8091
North-West England	(061 246) 8091
Northern Ireland	(0232) 8091
Oxon, Berks and Bucks	(0734) 8091
Somerset and Avon	(0793) 8091
South-West Midlands	(0452) 8091
South Yorks and the Peak District	(0742) 8091
Sussex coast	(01 246) 8097
West Yorks	(0532) 8091

For other areas or for personal advice, call the Meteorological Office: (01 836) 4311.

Safety and Comfort at Sea

Keeping in mind your safety and comfort can make all the difference between an enjoyable trip and a nightmare.

Clothing

Always be prepared for changes in weather, making sure you have waterproofs and extra warm clothing to hand. Boat anglers especially may find that a gentle breeze ashore becomes a chilly, stiff wind a few miles out.

Lights

Both boat and shore anglers should carry a good, strong battery lamp or windproof fuel lamp to see and be seen at night.

Boatman's word is law

Do not try to argue a skipper into taking you out if the weather is risky. Very often a sheltered alternative mark can be found, or, if the trip is postponed, a bit of jetty or shore fishing may not be time wasted. Afloat, accept the skipper's direction without argument, since he usually has your safety and comfort in mind – he wants you to come back for another trip, after all.

Conduct afloat

Do not jam up a boat with an over-large party which will lead to arguments over fishing space and much frustration with crossed lines. Every angler should make sure that the deck does not be cluttered with gear, and that slipper rags etc. are kept off the decking.

Small-boat safety

A boat of 12 feet or less should n risked out of sheltered water. In s boat, standing up risks capsize in a

Small-boat safety equipment

The following gear should be carr all times. If it is kept in a locker, the should be unlocked before your tri

A compass and chart for the f area.

A good strong torch.

A bell or horn for sounding in whistle is an alternative).

For close-in trips: red hand-held (ensure water-tight).

Offshore trips, coastal: red tw signal flares plus white flares (co warning is given with white flare).

Offshore trips, deep-sea: red para rockets plus white flares.

Anchor with strong warp and spare anchor.

First-aid box.

Lifejackets or lifebuoys for all a or raft.

Tell someone of your trip

Let somebody know where you are and, most importantly, when you e to return or make another port. Preferably this should be a harbour official.

Anchor safely
Keep your anchor buoyed and be prepared to slip it in an emergency. Do not anchor in shipping lanes or in places likely to be busy with marine traffic, or in half-hidden positions behind headlands where you might be surprised by a frigate rounding the corner.

Keep eyes open
All aboard are responsible for keeping watch for approaching shipping or signs of approaching bad weather.

Flares to be used in emergency
Danger of collision: fire white flare towards approaching vessel.

Distress, inshore: use red hand flare.

Distress, 3 to 7 miles offshore: fire red two-star signal flare. Repeat within two minutes. As help approaches, guide with red hand flare.

Distress, 7 miles or more offshore: fire red parachute rocket flare. Repeat within two minutes. Guide rescuers with hand-held flares.

Lights to be shown at night
Boats under oars: a white, hand-held torch.

Power vessels under 7 metres long with speed of under 7 knots: white, all-round light on mast (the higher the better, to avoid glare spoiling night vision). For additional safety, port and starboard sidelights.

Vessels under 50 metres at anchor: white, all-round light on mast. For additional safety port and starboard sidelights.

Range of lights in normal visibility is 1 mile with a 10-watt bulb and over 2 miles with a 25-watt bulb.

Coastguard services Always go to the assistance of anyone in distress at sea. If competent help has already arrived, heave to well away from the action until it is clear that no further assistance is needed.

Ashore, if you sight a distress signal, dial the coastguard immediately on the 999 emergency line and give the position of the light as exactly as possible.

At sea, if you have transmission ability, report radio distress signals to shore as well as trying to respond.

Rescue stations (MRCC = Marine Rescue Coordination Centre: MRSC = Marine Rescue Sub-Centre)

MRCC Aberdeen	(0224) 52334	MRSC Thames	Frinton-on-Sea
MRSC Shetland	Lerwick (0595) 2976		(025 56) 5518
MRSC Orkney	Kirkwall (0856) 3268	MRCC Dover	(0304) 852515
MRSC Wick	Kirkwall (0856) 2332	MRSC Shoreham	(079 17) 2226
MRSC Moray	Peterhead (0779) 4278	MRSC Solent	Freshwater (0983)
MRSC Forth	Crail (033 35) 666		752265
MRSC Tyne	North Shields (0632)	MRSC Portland	(0305) 820441
	572691	MRCC Brixham	(080 45) 2156
MRSC Tees	Redcar (0642) 476639	MRSC Falmouth	(0326) 314481
MRSC Humber	Spurn Point (096 46)	MRSC Land's End	Sennen (073 687)
	351		351
MRCC Yarmouth	(0493) 51338	MRSC Hartland	(023 74) 235

MRCC Swansea	(0792) 66534	MRCC Clyde	Greenock (0475) 29988
MRSC Milford Haven		MRSC Ramsey	(0624) 813255
	Dale (064 65) 218	MRSC Belfast	Groomsport (024 784)
MRSC Holyhead	(0407) 2051		284
MRSC Liverpool	Formby (070 48)	MRSC Oban	(0631) 63720
	72903	MRSC Stornoway	(0851) 2013

Organizations of Interest to the Sea Angler

The individual addresses of sea-fishing clubs and associations within the British Isles have not been given in this guide. They do not control waters, as freshwater fishing clubs do, but exist as social and organizational bodies offering different facilities to their members, and often a range of competitive events.

Many such clubs are affiliated to the National Federation of Sea Anglers (NFSA), whose main office and regional secretaries will be able to supply the addresses of many local sea-fishing clubs (a stamped, addressed envelope with such inquiries is essential).

The National Federation of Sea Anglers

The NFSA represents around 2 million sea anglers and more than 800 sea-angling clubs and is open to individual and club or association membership. It is recognized by the Sports Council as a representative of the sport.

Besides this, it runs a series of fishing festivals at national and regional levels, and the medal award scheme for specimen fish caught around Britain. There is a national secretariat and regional (divisional) committees and secretaries.

The national Secretary and Treasurer is R. W. Page, 26 Downsview Crescent, Uckfield, Sussex, TN22 1UB. Tel. Uckfield 3589. Divisional secretaries are:

Cornwall: A. Blewett, 6 Gloucester Road, Newlyn, Penzance.

Essex: J. Saunders, 16 Retreat Road, Westcliff-on-Sea.

Isle of Wight: R. E. Winship, Robreena, West Hill Road, Ryde, IoW.

North-West: V. O'Brien, 80 Lumn Road, Hyde, Greater Manchester.

Severn: C. Jones, 11 Longway Avenue, Whitchurch, Bristol.

South-East: R. Harrison, Pytchcroft, Ashford Road, Chartham, Canterbury, Kent.

Southern: W. Dyer, 5 Northfield Close, Seaford, Sussex.

Wales: Mrs C. Davies, 71 Heol Powis, Birchgrove, Cardiff.

Wessex: W. Rawles, 58 Sycamore Avenue, Hiltingbury, Chandler's Ford, Hants.

Wyvern: W. Hern, 29 West Hill Road, Torquay, Devon.

Yorkshire: J. Amery, 34 Mallom Avenue, Euxton, Chorley, Lancs.

The Anglers' Cooperative Association

Fights pollution cases on behalf of anglers, supported entirely by voluntary contributions (K. Sutton, Chief Executive, Midland Bank Chambers, Westgate, Grantham, Lincs).

The National Anglers' Council

Represents the freshwater and sea sides

of the sport to government bodies, administers the British Record (rod-caught) Fish Committee (P. H. Tombleson, 11 Cowgate, Peterborough).

The Bass Anglers Sport Fishing Society
J. Churchouse, Rishon, Longfield Road, Weymouth, Dorset.

The British Conger Club
R. Quest, 5 Hill Crest, Mannamead, Plymouth.

The British Light Tackle Club
R. Rush, 7 Southcote Road, Tufnell Park, London N19.

The National Mullet Club
G. Green, 53 Downlands Close, Bexhill-on-Sea, Sussex.

The Shark Angling Club of Great Britain
J. Tudor, Jolly Sailor Inn, W. Looe, Cornwall.

The Irish Federation of Sea Anglers
H. O'Rorke, 67 Windsor Drive, Monkstown, Co. Dublin.

The Scottish Federation of Sea Anglers
Mrs C. Watson, 18 Ainslie Place, Edinburgh.

The Welsh Federation of Sea Anglers
G. S. Howen, 11 Stafford Road, Newport, Gwent.

The British Record (rod-caught) Fish Committee
As National Anglers' Council (see above).

The International Game Fishing Association
3000 E. Las Olas Boulevard, Fort Lauderdale, Florida 33316, USA.

The Northern Ireland Tourist Board
River House, High Street, Belfast.

The Irish Tourist Board (Bord Failte)
Baggot Street Bridge, Dublin 2.

Record fish bodies
Records for England and Northern Ireland are dealt with by the British Record (rod-caught) Fish Committee through the National Anglers' Council (address above). Claims through the Scottish Federation of Sea Anglers and the Welsh Record Fish Committee are forwarded to the British Record (rod-caught) Fish Committee. Claims for Eire records should be made to the Irish Specimen Fish Committee, Balnagowan, Mobhi Boreen, Glasnevin, Dublin 9.

Baits

Many of the baits used by the sea angler may be collected either before a trip or during fishing; and in addition many tackle dealers nowadays sell fresh baits.

Lugworm

These plump, fleshy worms inhabit sandy and muddy ground which is covered by water at high tide. The colour varies from black to brown and greenish-brown.

Telltale signs are the worms' casts, or little piles of sand, and if the area is inspected carefully there are nearby also small holes, the other end of a U-shaped tunnel averaging about a foot in depth. At low tide the worm is usually in part of this tunnel, and when digging is sensed it will withdraw to the bottom of the U. Dig between the cast and exit hole.

Lugworm may be kept in a roll of dry newspaper for a few days – this helps to toughen them up.

Ragworm

The ragworm inhabits muddy, sandy, stony or weedy ground, where it can be collected by shallow digging, overturning boulders (please return to original place) or lifting clumps of weed. Keep in newspaper or a container of dry sand for two or three days at most. Ragworm can be long, and they have a fringe or frill of filaments along each side of their body with a pair of nippers at the head end (these can deliver a nip). Colour varies from red to greeny-brown.

Fresh fish

The mackerel is one of the most obliging bait fish, and often a good number can be caught on a trip before fishing commences. If mackerel have proved scarce inshore, take some fishmongers' fish or freeze your own for a constant supply.

Other fish which give reasonable results are fresh or frozen sprats, whitebait, herring (rather soft) and pilchards. Strips ('lasks') of mackerel and other fish are made by first slicing the flank of the fish off the bone, starting with the knife from the head end. This flank can then be laid on a cutting board and trimmed to the size required.

Sandeels

An excellent bait, used either live, freshly killed or frozen for bass and turbot. They inhabit sandy beaches with surf and are rather localized in occurrence, playing and feeding until the tide recedes and then burying themselves quickly. They can be caught with a handnet, but professional collectors use a net which incorporates a rake along the lower edge, so that fish which are burying themselves are pushed up and into the net. Usually used whole.

Peeler crab, softbacks

Before the crab moults its skin, which it does a number of times during its growth, it is known as a peeler. When the old shell comes away it leaves the crab with a soft skin for a little while, when it is known as a softback. In both these stages it is rather unprotected and will hide, emerging when the shell has toughened. The place to search is beneath boulders, in crevices, and under weed masses at low tide. Many fish are especially fond of peeler and softback crabs, which perhaps smell different from those with hardened shells. The hermit crab, which inhabits the shells of whelks and other shellfish, also has a soft body and makes an attractive bait – without the shell, of course.

Mussels, razorfish etc.

Shellfish flesh attracts a range of species, especially flatfish and cod. Mussels adhere to pier piles, rocks etc., and large specimens can be broken away from the clumps for bait. It helps to open a few shells before fishing, allowing the flesh to dry a little and toughen up. Razorfish live buried near the low tide mark on sandy beaches, leaving a funnel-like depression. Several clam relatives do the same, some of them shooting a squirt of water in the air as you approach the holes. They can be dug up and shelled for bait, attracting flatfish, bass, cod and a number of other species. No useful preserving methods.

Squid

More and more fresh squid is appearing in our fish shops as a result of changing tastes. It should be bought when available and frozen if not needed immediately. The flesh can be cut into strips for smaller species, while for big cod, for instance, the whole head or a sizeable chunk of flesh can be used. Because it is also very tough, pieces of squid are used to hold softer baits like worms on the hook.

MAPS

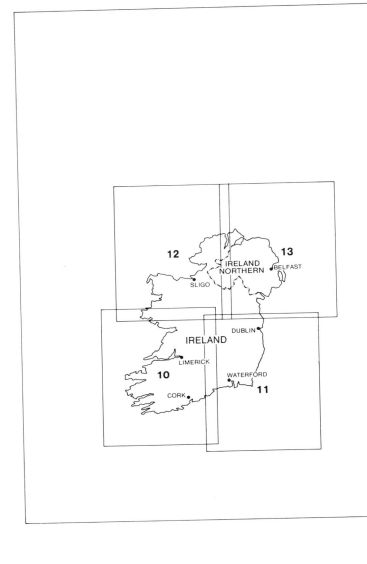

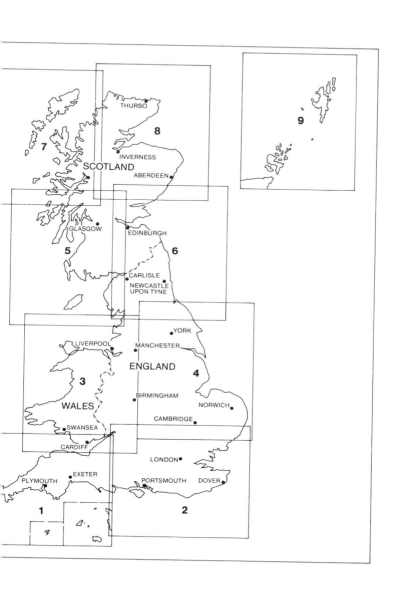

THURSO

8

7

INVERNESS

SCOTLAND

ABERDEEN

GLASGOW

EDINBURGH

5

6

CARLISLE

NEWCASTLE
UPON TYNE

YORK

LIVERPOOL

MANCHESTER

ENGLAND

3

4

BIRMINGHAM

WALES

NORWICH

SWANSEA

CAMBRIDGE

CARDIFF

LONDON

PLYMOUTH

EXETER

PORTSMOUTH

DOVER

1

2

9

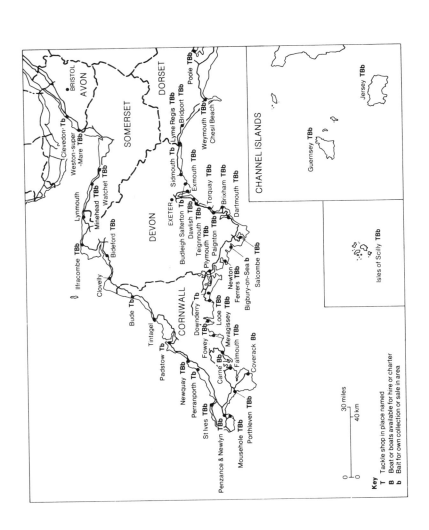

Key

T Tackle shop in place named

B Boat or boats available for hire or charter

b Bait for own collection or sale in area

0 ⌐ 30 miles
0 ⌐ 40 km

Ilfracombe **TBb**

Lynmouth

Minehead **TBb**

Watchet **TBb**

Weston-super-Mare **TBb**

Clevedon· **Tb**

BRISTOL

AVON

SOMERSET

Clovelly

Bideford **TBb**

DEVON

EXETER

Sidmouth **Tb**

Budleigh Salterton **Tb**

Lyme Regis **TBb**

Bridport **TBb**

Poole **TBb**

DORSET

Exmouth **TBb**

Dawlish **TBb**

Teignmouth **TBb**

Weymouth **TBb**

Chesil Beach

Torquay **TBb**

Paignton **TBb**

Brixham **TBb**

Dartmouth **TBb**

Plymouth **TBb**

Newton
Ferrers **TBb**

Bigbury-on-Sea **b**

Salcombe **TBb**

Bude **Tb**

Tintagel

Padstow **TBb**

Newquay **TBb**

Perranporth **Tb**

Downderry **Tb**

Looe **TBb**

Fowey **TBb**

Mevagissey **TBb**

Carné **Bb**

Falmouth **TBb**

Coverack **Bb**

CORNWALL

St Ives **TBb**

Penzance & Newlyn **TBb**

Mousehole **TBb**

Porthleven **TBb**

Isles of Scilly **TBb**

CHANNEL ISLANDS

Guernsey **TBb**

Jersey **TBb**

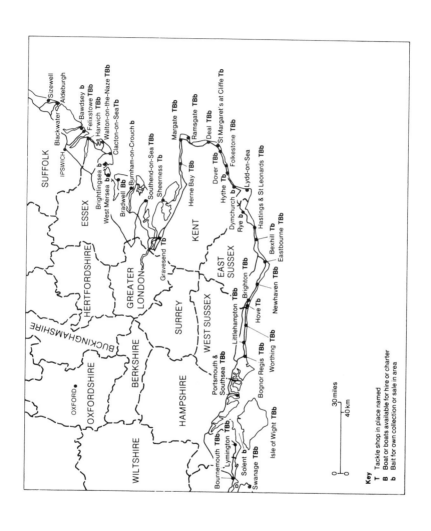

Key

T Tackle shop in place named
B Boat or boats available for hire or charter
b Bait for own collection or sale in area

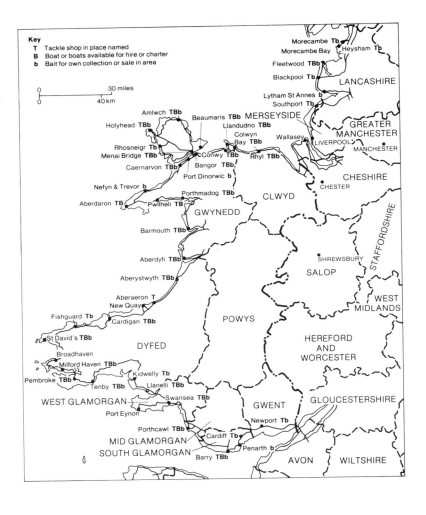

Key

T   Tackle shop in place named
B   Boat or boats available for hire or charter
b   Bait for own collection or sale in area

0   30 miles
0   40 km

Morecambe **Tb**
Morecambe Bay   Heysham **Tb**
Fleetwood **TBb**
Blackpool **Tb**   LANCASHIRE
Lytham St Annes **b**
Southport **Tb**   GREATER
          MANCHESTER

Amlwch **TBb**   Beaumaris **TBb**   MERSEYSIDE
Holyhead **TBb**   Llandudno **TBb**
           Colwyn   Wallasey   LIVERPOOL
Rhosneigr **Tb**   Bay **TBb**   MANCHESTER
Menai Bridge **TBb**   Conwy **TBb**   Rhyl **TBb**
Caernarvon **TBb**   Bangor **TBb**
          Port Dinorwic **b**   CHESHIRE
Nefyn & Trevor **b**   CHESTER
        Porthmadog **TBb**   CLWYD
Aberdaron **TB**   Pwllheli **TB**
               GWYNEDD

Barmouth **TBb**
                        STAFFORDSHIRE
Aberdyfi **TBb**   SHREWSBURY
Aberystwyth **TBb**   SALOP
                       WEST
Aberaeron **T**   MIDLANDS
New Quay
Fishguard **Tb**   POWYS
      Cardigan **TBb**
St David's **TBb**   HEREFORD
Broadhaven   DYFED   AND
Milford Haven **TBb**   WORCESTER
Pembroke **TBb**   Kidwelly **Tb**
    Tenby **TBb**   Llanelli **TBb**
             Swansea **TBb**   GLOUCESTERSHIRE
WEST GLAMORGAN   GWENT
Port Eynon   Newport **Tb**
Porthcawl **TBb**   AVON   WILTSHIRE
MID GLAMORGAN   Cardiff **Tb**
SOUTH GLAMORGAN   Penarth **b**
        Barry **TBb**

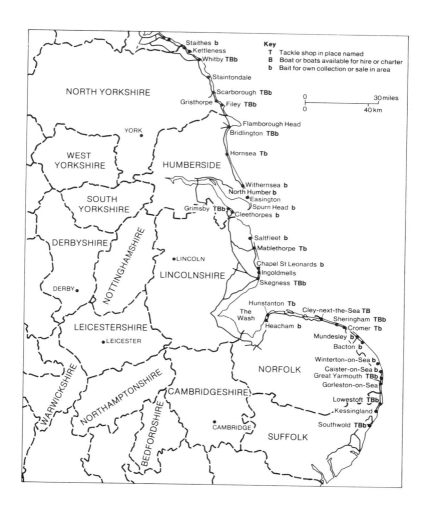

Key
T Tackle shop in place named
B Boat or boats available for hire or charter
b Bait for own collection or sale in area

Staithes **b**
Kettleness
Whitby **TBb**

Staintondale

NORTH YORKSHIRE

Scarborough **TBb**
Gristhorpe Filey **TBb**

YORK

Flamborough Head
Bridlington **TBb**

WEST YORKSHIRE

HUMBERSIDE

Hornsea **Tb**

Withernsea **b**
North Humber **b**
Easington
Spurn Head **b**

SOUTH YORKSHIRE

Grimsby **TBb**
Cleethorpes **b**

DERBYSHIRE

Saltfleet **b**
Mablethorpe **Tb**

LINCOLN

Chapel St Leonards **b**
Ingoldmells
Skegness **TBb**

LINCOLNSHIRE

DERBY

NOTTINGHAMSHIRE

Hunstanton **Tb**
The Wash
Heacham **b**

Cley-next-the-Sea **TB**
Sheringham **TBb**
Cromer **Tb**
Mundesley **b**
Bacton **b**

LEICESTERSHIRE

LEICESTER

Winterton-on-Sea **b**
Caister-on-Sea **b**
Great Yarmouth **TBb**
Gorleston-on-Sea

NORFOLK

WARWICKSHIRE

NORTHAMPTONSHIRE

CAMBRIDGESHIRE

BEDFORDSHIRE

Lowestoft **TBb**
Kessingland
Southwold **TBb**

CAMBRIDGE

SUFFOLK

0   30 miles
0   40 km

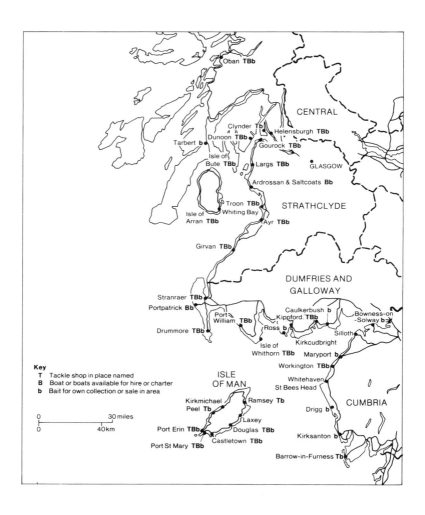

Oban **TBb**

CENTRAL

Clynder **Tb**
Helensburgh **TBb**
Dunoon **TBb**
Tarbert **b**
Gourock **TBb**
Isle of
Bute **TBb**
Largs **TBb**
GLASGOW
Ardrossan & Saltcoats **Bb**

STRATHCLYDE

Troon **TBb**
Whiting Bay
Isle of
Arran **TBb**
Ayr **TBb**

Girvan **TBb**

DUMFRIES AND
GALLOWAY

Stranraer **TBb**
Portpatrick **Bb**
Port
William **TBb**
Caulkerbush **b**
Kippford. **TBb**
Bowness-on
-Solway **b**
Ross **b**
Silloth
Drummore **TBb**
Kirkcudbright
Isle of
Whithorn **TBb**
Maryport **b**
Workington **TBb**
Whitehaven
St Bees Head

Key
T   Tackle shop in place named
B   Boat or boats available for hire or charter
b   Bait for own collection or sale in area

ISLE
OF MAN

CUMBRIA

Kirkmichael
Peel **Tb**
Ramsey **Tb**
Drigg **b**

0 ——————— 30 miles
0 ——————— 40km

Laxey
Port Erin **TBb**
Douglas **TBb**
Kirksanton **b**
Port St Mary **TBb**
Castletown **TBb**

Barrow-in-Furness **Tb**

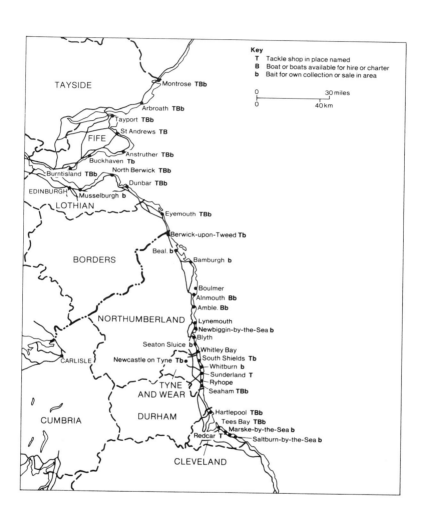

Key
T Tackle shop in place named
B Boat or boats available for hire or charter
b Bait for own collection or sale in area

0   30 miles
0   40 km

TAYSIDE

Montrose **TBb**

Arbroath **TBb**

Tayport **TBb**

St Andrews **TB**

FIFE

Anstruther **TBb**

Buckhaven **Tb**

North Berwick **TBb**

Burntisland **TBb**

Dunbar **TBb**

EDINBURGH

Musselburgh **b**

LOTHIAN

Eyemouth **TBb**

Berwick-upon-Tweed **Tb**

Beal. **b**

BORDERS

Bamburgh **b**

Boulmer

Alnmouth **Bb**

Amble. **Bb**

NORTHUMBERLAND

Lynemouth

Newbiggin-by-the-Sea **b**

Blyth

Seaton Sluice **b**

Whitley Bay

CARLISLE

South Shields **Tb**

Newcastle on Tyne **Tb**

Whitburn **b**

Sunderland **T**

Ryhope

TYNE AND WEAR

Seaham **TBb**

DURHAM

Hartlepool **TBb**

CUMBRIA

Tees Bay **TBb**

Marske-by-the-Sea **b**

Redcar **T**

Saltburn-by-the-Sea **b**

CLEVELAND

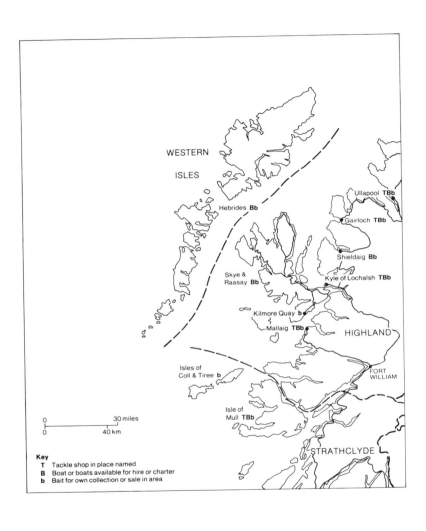

WESTERN

ISLES

Ullapool **TBb**

Gairloch **TBb**

Hebrides **Bb**

Shieldaig **Bb**

Kyle of Lochalsh **TBb**

Skye &
Raasay **Bb**

Kilmore Quay **b**

Mallaig **TBb**

HIGHLAND

Isles of
Coll & Tiree **b**

FORT
WILLIAM

Isle of
Mull **TBb**

STRATHCLYDE

0 ———— 30 miles
0 ———— 40 km

Key

T Tackle shop in place named
B Boat or boats available for hire or charter
b Bait for own collection or sale in area

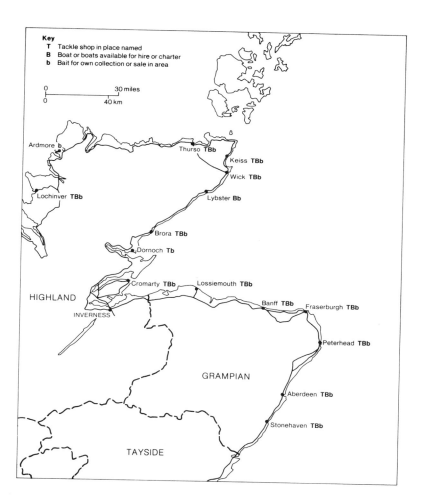

Key
T   Tackle shop in place named
B   Boat or boats available for hire or charter
b   Bait for own collection or sale in area

0   30 miles
0   40 km

Ardmore **b**

Thurso **TBb**

Keiss **TBb**

Wick **TBb**

Lochinver **TBb**

Lybster **Bb**

Brora **TBb**

Dornoch **Tb**

Cromarty **TBb**

Lossiemouth **TBb**

HIGHLAND

Banff **TBb**

Fraserburgh **TBb**

INVERNESS

Peterhead **TBb**

GRAMPIAN

Aberdeen **TBb**

Stonehaven **TBb**

TAYSIDE

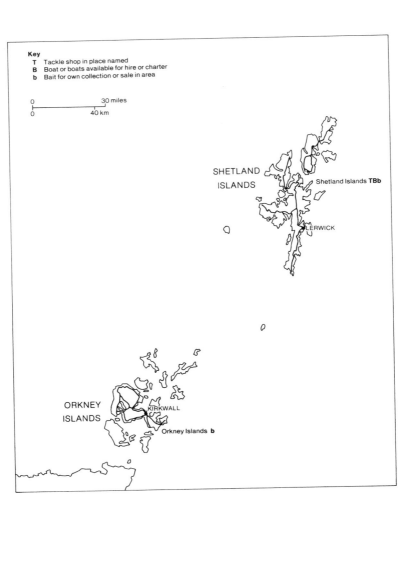

Key
T Tackle shop in place named
B Boat or boats available for hire or charter
b Bait for own collection or sale in area

0   30 miles
0   40 km

SHETLAND
ISLANDS

Shetland Islands **TBb**

LERWICK

ORKNEY
ISLANDS

KIRKWALL

Orkney Islands **b**

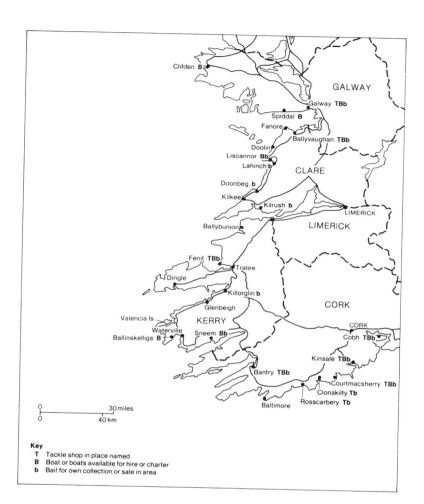

Clifden **B**

GALWAY

Galway **TBb**

Spiddal **B**

Fanore

Ballyvaughan **TBb**

Doolin

Liscannor **Bb**

Lahinch **b**

CLARE

Doonbeg **b**

Kilkee

Kilrush **b**

LIMERICK

Ballybunion

LIMERICK

Fenit **TBb**

Tralee

Dingle

Killorglin **b**

Glenbeigh

CORK

Valencia Is.

KERRY

CORK

Waterville

Cobh **TBb**

Sneem **Bb**

Ballinskelligs **B**

Kinsale **TBb**

Bantry **TBb**

Courtmacsherry **TBb**

Clonakilty **Tb**

Rosscarbery **Tb**

Baltimore

| 0 | | 30 miles |
| 0 | | 40 km |

Key

T   Tackle shop in place named
B   Boat or boats available for hire or charter
b   Bait for own collection or sale in area

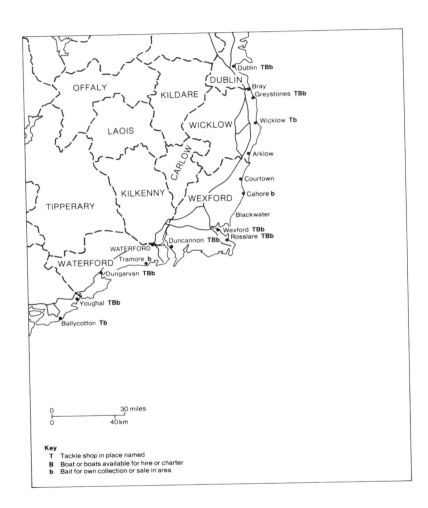

Dublin **TBb**

DUBLIN

OFFALY

KILDARE

Bray
Greystones **TBb**

LAOIS

WICKLOW

Wicklow **Tb**

Arklow

CARLOW

Courtown

Cahore **b**

TIPPERARY

KILKENNY

WEXFORD

Blackwater

Wexford **TBb**
Rosslare **TBb**

Duncannon **TBb**

WATERFORD

Tramore **b**

WATERFORD

Dungarvan **TBb**

Youghal **TBb**

Ballycotton **Tb**

0 ———————— 30 miles
0 ———————— 40 km

Key

T   Tackle shop in place named
B   Boat or boats available for hire or charter
b   Bait for own collection or sale in area

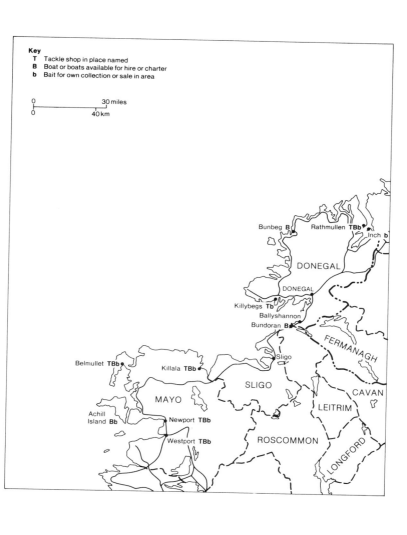

Key
- **T** Tackle shop in place named
- **B** Boat or boats available for hire or charter
- **b** Bait for own collection or sale in area

0   30 miles
0   40 km

Bunbeg **B**

Rathmullen **TBb**

Inch **b**

DONEGAL

DONEGAL

Killybegs **Tb**

Ballyshannon

Bundoran **B**

FERMANAGH

Sligo

Belmullet **TBb**

Killala **TBb**

SLIGO

CAVAN

MAYO

LEITRIM

Achill
Island **Bb**

Newport **TBb**

Westport **TBb**

ROSCOMMON

LONGFORD

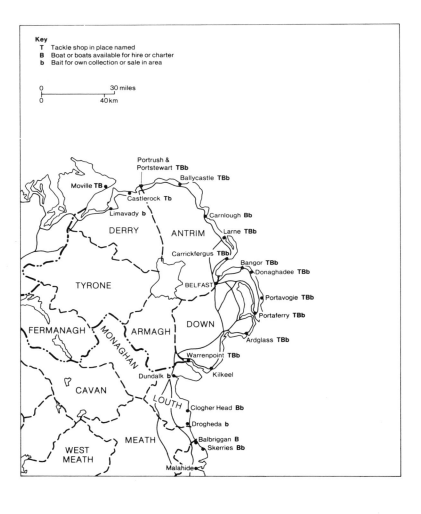

Key
T Tackle shop in place named
B Boat or boats available for hire or charter
b Bait for own collection or sale in area

0   30 miles
0   40 km

Portrush &
Portstewart **TBb**
Ballycastle **TBb**
Moville **TB**
Castlerock **Tb**
Carnlough **Bb**
Limavady **b**
DERRY
ANTRIM
Larne **TBb**
Carrickfergus **TBb**
Bangor **TBb**
Donaghadee **TBb**
BELFAST
Portavogie **TBb**
TYRONE
Portaferry **TBb**
DOWN
FERMANAGH
MONAGHAN
ARMAGH
Ardglass **TBb**
Warrenpoint **TBb**
Dundalk **b**
Kilkeel
CAVAN
LOUTH
Clogher Head **Bb**
Drogheda **b**
MEATH
Balbriggan **B**
Skerries **Bb**
WEST
MEATH
Malahide